PRAISE FOR THE AUTHOR

This book gives a different take on goal setting from the books I've seen so far. It brings in new ideas and examples, and covers many techniques that actually work for people setting goals. Many of these are techniques I use in skiing, and in life. Chris talks about goals, why they are important, and how to properly set them. He also writes about the importance of path, visualization, mentors, techniques for achieving and overcoming failure, the importance of responsibility, and even timing of when to reveal your goals to others.

Winning the slalom World Cup title was my goal from the beginning of the 2012/2013 race season. The World Championships title was incredible, but it wasn't the goal that I had set. It was a stepping-stone on the path to my goal. In order to win the World Cup title, I had to perform at my top level in every single race that season – I was careful about putting any one race above another in importance, because that would change my focus to being oriented around individual races, rather than my goal that season. I tried to think of the World Championships as another normal race, even though it is the most prestigious event in World Cup skiing aside from the Olympics. At the end of the season I considered winning the gold at the World Championships as one of my greatest accomplishments, but because it wasn't what I had set out to do, I saw it as a bonus – cherry on top of the very sweet cake that was my entire season.

My overall goal, my dream, is to be a great skier winning in all of the different events. I believe that people create their own luck. The most successful people in the world have had their fair share of suffering, obstacles, and hard work, and were able to rise above it all because they set goals and put in the effort to prepare. For me, slalom has been a part of the process of creating my own luck, or creating my own miracle.

Visualization plays a huge role in my improvement and performance. In training I use technical queues and imagine myself skiing the perfect turn around each gate. In competition, I focus on the feeling I have gotten from training when I ski that perfect turn, and that feeling drives me down the course, allowing me to free my mind without being mindless. When my mind is free, my muscles take over. All of my preparation to that point is brought to the forefront, and I just know what to do. I dream about skiing and I feel it every day. Have I had some failures? Yes, I have, but being a champion is about overcoming failures, facing adversity and then winning. Winning doesn't always mean gold. Winning is when you set your mind to a goal, and you accomplish it.

I have many goals, but I don't talk about all of them to everyone. Some might seem too lofty, arrogant, or downright crazy to other people. There are times to reveal your goals and times to keep them to yourself.

My parents have been my mentors, teaching me to be the best I can be. Winning has come as a product of always striving to be my best. I have had some great coaches and I've watched and analyzed many awesome skiers in my career – those mentors have played a huge part in my success and achievements.

As a 21 year old, it's really important to me to connect with the younger kids. I like to get some time face-to-face with them to show them that I'm not actually that different from them. Chris uses examples through his book to show how achievers are people just like you, and achievements like theirs are accessible to you as well.

Whatever your goal, this book will give you approaches to setting goals that you can tailor to your own beliefs, personality, and motivation and help you create your own miracle. Have fun with it!

Mikaela Shiffrin, Reigning Olympic, World Cup, and World Champion Slalom Skier

---

As an athlete, author, real estate investor and business owner, I have been setting goals – consciously or unconsciously – all my life. Because I love finding new and better ways of doing things, I was naturally intrigued by the concept of *"Goal Setting for People Who Can't Set Goals."* I was delighted to discover so many new and interesting approaches to achieving goals and I learned a great deal. It is an entertaining read, well researched with pertinent anecdotes. Chris

Christoff succeeds in demystifying the art of goal setting and offers easy to follow, proven and practical steps for achieving your heart's desire. Reading his book can change your life!

Joanne Verikios, Entrepreneur, Horse Breeder, Trainer and Judge, Award-Winning Athlete, Investor, International Author of "*Winning Horsemanship*"

This book is a must read for anyone who wants more out of life. This could be business-related or personal. What makes Chris's book stand out is how it covers every angle of Goal Setting. So many books these days are abstract and focus on theory alone without any real world examples. Chris uses his own experiences and those of many others throughout the book to highlight his points. This brings them to life, makes them real and shows us how we can use them to improve our own lives. He also backs this up by quoting experts in a range of fields. What stood out for me was the chapter on overcoming fear and particularly this quote, "Challenges are not in the way, they are on the way to any goal." Read this book. You'll be pleased you did.

Pete Burdon, Media Trainer,
International Author of "*Media Training for Modern Leaders*"

This book is the ultimate goal setting manual. You will discover a different way of looking at goal setting, preparing for goal setting and your path towards your goals. Chris Christoff approaches goal setting from all angles and will give you the best possible chance of reaching yours.

Sharon Davey, Author of "*Awesome Careers for Gen Ys*"

More success, more abundance, more health doesn't just 'happen.' We have to create them.

When we set goals, we begin the first creation. Anthony Robbins says, "*Setting a goal is the first step in turning the invisible into the visible.*"

In this book, Chris Christoff has put together gems of his proven tools and techniques of 'Goal Setting' into an accessible read. He not only teaches you how to take the 'first step' but includes many practical and smart steps to manifest your goals and help you achieve anything you want. A must read for anyone serious about creating a meaningful and successful life.

Selina Seah, The Energy Alchemist, Founder and Director of The Aura Chakra Company, Success Strategist Coach

---

Having known Chris for 20 years, it is a privilege for me to write this testimonial. Chris has achieved some amazing things in his life and this book reflects exactly how you can do the same. My favorite chapter is *Visualizing Your Goals The Art of Thinkualization*. As a personal trainer, I have personally benefited from reading this as I use Chris's techniques with my clients. In fact, it positively excites me as I also use his methods for my personal goals. It is a realistic and lively read and is based on Chris's own personal achievements. I have had the pleasure of having many firsthand conversations with Chris on this subject and am always fascinated with Chris's passion for motivating others.

You will definitely be better for reading this book!

John Briggs, Director and Trainer, Inspire Success Academy of Fitness

---

Bad news makes headlines, sending fear and uncertainty into our lives, just like being paralyzed by fear of failure or rejection through our own insecurities. Chris shares his experience and knowledge in setting personal goals through visualization; he understands setting goals and meeting deadlines can induce stress.

This book is a must read. Chris's book paves a clear path and helps you through that maze of pressure to have the life, relationships and health that you sometimes feel you don't deserve at all. He clarifies any uncertainty and doubt.

His simple techniques on setting goals and the steps to achieve them will change your life forever.

Coral Brian Wheatley, Author, Investor, Boutique Developer, Mum, Share Trader, Author of "*Building Wealth in a Self-Managed Super Fund – How I Turned 80K into 4 Million and How You Can Too*"

When Chris invited me to write a comment for his latest book, we had never met, nor have we known each other from past "lives"; however, the word mirrors the man, having now dipped into the text of this brand new work, "*Goal Setting for People Who Can't Set Goals*."

This book is a must-read!

Not only does Chris reveal, with rigorous scrutiny, our recurring blocks and barriers to successfully achieving our goals, he offers clearly, simply and professionally, a way through, under and around them. Each chapter is systematically formulated to steer the reader to right and logical action.

The text is colored with nuggets and hot tips for consistent progress … in the office, studio; sportsground, classroom or family nest.

Chris's examples are convincingly researched and sewn together with an obvious practical insight into the elusive nuances of human emotions and the subconscious. "*Goal Setting for People Who Can't Set Goals*" is an open-and-read-anywhere gem … great for a quick, working reference. You won't just want this book; you will decide you need it.

Steve Coleman, Director CDN21Pty Ltd, Outdoor Educator, Children's Author, Author of "*Decisions, Decisions! How to Make the Right One Every Time*"

Fear of failure, or fear of success, is the emotion that is usually linked to questions that we have no answers to. It is the "What if?" emotion that can consume us. It is a natural part of processing a situation that is new to us, common in goal setting. We know that. What we didn't know until this book was how to control it and take the fear out of feeling fear. This book will give you strategies to do just that. Easy to read, practical advice and you will finish reading this book with the tools to control your fear, and master your achievement.

Fiona Lane, Author, Speaker, Children's Services and Grief Counsellor, Author of ***"Surviving the Hurt: A Practical Guide to Overcoming All Types of Grief and Loss"***

GOAL
SETTING
FOR PEOPLE WHO
CAN'T SET GOALS

GLOBAL
PUBLISHING
G R O U P

Global Publishing Group
Australia • New Zealand • Singapore • America • London

GOAL SETTING

FOR PEOPLE WHO CAN'T SET GOALS

PROVEN TOOLS AND TECHNIQUES TO
ACHIEVE ANYTHING YOU WANT

CHRIS CHRISTOFF

First Edition 2016

National Library of Australia
Cataloguing-in-Publication entry:

Creator: Christoff, Chris, author.

Goal Setting for People Who Can't Set Goals : Proven Tools and Techniques to Achieve Anything You Want / Chris Christoff.

1st ed.
ISBN: 9781925288063 (paperback)

Goal (Psychology)
Motivation (Psychology)
Self-actualization (Psychology)
Self-help techniques.
Success.

Dewey Number: 153.8

Published by Global Publishing Group
PO Box 517 Mt Evelyn, Victoria 3796 Australia
Email info@GlobalPublishingGroup.com.au

Printed in China

For further information about orders:
Phone: +61 3 9739 4686 or Fax +61 3 8648 6871

I dedicate this book to my family – to my wife, Karen, who supported me through my different life journeys and fed me while I locked myself away in my office writing this book. To my children Christopher, Sabrina and Joash, who believed their Dad could do it. It makes me proud that I made them proud. To my mum, Marjorie, who, at 82 years of age, is still on her journey of exploration and learning. To my dad, Chris, thank you for the conversations and the advice.

I also dedicate this book to you, those who want more from life and are actively seeking to learn how to achieve it, those who have tried the customarily taught goal setting techniques and are looking for methods they can mold to themselves, and those who believe there must be more to achieving than trying to wish something into existence. You inspire me!

Chris Christoff

ACKNOWLEDGEMENTS

When I thought about who I would like to write the forward for my book I decided on someone in the property industry, the industry of my passion, after spending 30 years in information technology. There is no one as successful as Harry Triguboff, who came to Australia in 1960 and navigated the roller coaster of the Australian property development industry with eminent success. Thank you, Mr. Triguboff.

Meg Kerr, thank you for the many hours you spent with my manuscript, correcting it and making it more readable, with a skilled and practiced eye. Thank you for the Spanish language tips, my little side project.

Joash Christoff, my youngest, for being a sounding board for ideas, phrases, the English language and finding "just the right word."

Marc Miles and Jessica Oey, thank you for allowing me to bounce my ideas off you, for testing some of them out in your lives and for making me structure my ideas so that I could explain them articulately. I know I will be celebrating the great achievements of your respective journeys with you.

Carolyn Cranwell, we met at the first author's workshop and we have been great friends since. Thank you for the conversations, ideas and guidance. Thank you for the strength and clarity you bring to writing and I wish you much success with your book, *"Navigating Alzheimer's Survival Secrets of a Long Term Carer."*

Thank you Darren Stephens and Jackie Tallentyre for the guidance, inspiration and knowledge, not just for the book, but also for the preparation to becoming an author and for the brilliant program you have built to guide authors to write and publish the books they have within them. Thank you to the team from Global Publishing Group who makes sure it all happens, and to Kelly Mayne, my book project manager, a special thank you for doing what a good project manager does and keeping me on track.

I also wish to acknowledge my mentors, both current and past. I have learned much and look to you for future learning and guidance in my various roles, in property as well as personal development. As promised, I will keep your anonymity you know who you are.

In my time on the path of self-development, I have attended many courses and sat through many seminars. Some of them provided me with the skills and knowledge to bring me to where I am today and, along with my own experiences, shaped my life. Some showed me how not to do it, some got me annoyed and some showed me what I should avoid. They all shaped my thinking, skills and my beliefs and I am grateful for all of them.

ACKNOWLEDGEMENT OF MY CONTRIBUTORS

I express the deepest thank you to those achievers who generously gave of their time for an interview and so openly discussed their achievements and failures, as well as their approaches to goal setting and goal achievement.

Gai Williams – The entrepreneurial pharmacist

Coral Brian-Wheatley – An inspirational journey in property investing

Joanne Verikios – Fellow author and property investor

Darren Morgan – Fair dinkum Aussie with a passion for top fuel motor racing

Paul Moni – Businessman extraordinaire, thank you for the guidance in a past life

Tiffany Mason – "*Don't be the prisoner of your past. Be the designer of your future*"

Dr. X – Thank you for your insights, keep up the important work

Sharon Jurd – Leadership in how to do it right

Kawena Gordon – A fun interview, a whole other world

John Gearon – How to shortcut direct to high performance

Tony Gattari – Driven with energy, masterful with people

Patricia Dennis – Experienced so much, accomplished so much more

Julius Czerny – There is this bloke, he had a heart attack, then did amazing things

Jacqui Christie – Jacqui, maybe there is something to this manifesting thing ☺

Donna Campisi – Lives her motto, "*There is no such thing as can't,*" a champion of fur buddies

Graham Bibby – Driven from a childhood passion, connected to the world

Thank you one, thank you all.

FREE BONUS GIFTS
Valued at $997 – Yours FREE!

I want to be your mentor and guide you through your goal-setting journey. This book will get you started; get you on the path. I have created some special items just for you, to help enhance the techniques you can use to achieve your goals. I also want to hear from you about what you learned from the book, about your own experiences with success and failure, what you did about them and what you gained.

You will find these BONUS resources, valued at $997, on our website:

www.YouCanSetGoals.com/Resources

- **BONUS #1** The audio and transcripts of interviews I conducted for the 'People Like You' guidance.

- **BONUS #2** eBook The Last Chapter – Information on asking, how to do an end-of-day reframing, the science behind gratitude, playing with the math of mental transmission and other interesting stuff.

- **BONUS #3** eBook Know Your Starting Point – Taking stock of where you are, working your personal assets and liabilities, identifying areas you can set goals, and how to reduce risk and turn it into work.

- **BONUS #4** eBook Comparing Yourself with Others – There is a right way and a wrong way. How to compare yourself productively with others, to develop traits and characteristics.

- **BONUS #5** eBook Manifesting or Visualizing? – My view of the concept referred to as manifesting.

…. And eBooks on mentors, procrastination, and more!

Claim your FREE BONUS GIFTS NOW by going to

www.YouCanSetGoals.com/Resources

To send me feedback on your experiences:

 www.facebook.com/YouCanSetGoals Feedback@YouCanSetGoals.com

CONTENTS

FOREWORD

Harry O. Triguboff, AO

Congratulations on investing in this book.

Being invited to write the foreword to Chris's book was an interesting request. You see, as far as I am concerned, I have never consciously set a goal in my life. I had to stop and think about it. I am always saying to people in my business, "*Whatever you start, you must finish.*" On reflection, I now see that everything with a start and finish has a goal in between. If each apartment I have built is representative of a single goal then we have achieved over 65,000 of them. I am far more qualified to speak of goal setting than I first thought.

The internet is full of amazing statistics on goal setting such as, 80% of the population never sets goals and 70% that do set them, fail to achieve them. There is so much we can do with our lives but many procrastinate and do nothing.

In this book, Chris explores the methods to achieve goals that go further than the "traditional" methods you read about. People do what they like doing. Setting and achieving goals should be enjoyable. The secret to achieving goals is to understand why you want them. The depth of your understanding about why you want something will dictate the work you put in, your response to the obstacles you have to overcome and the drive to go on when you feel you want to stop. I love what I do, I love to work both in my business and on my business and I have been doing it for over 50 years.

The success of Meriton rides on my ability to know what the market wants and my goal is to deliver what the market wants. When you are focused on your goal in the right way your subconscious will highlight the opportunities for you to realize the goal. Your ability to deliver will come from your preparedness and drive.

For me, goals and common sense go hand in hand. I was never taught to set goals at school or how to achieve them. It has been instinctive for me. I have a very big team of people working around me and I don't doubt I demand they set goals every minute of every day. If they did not, not only would our buildings not be built on time, they would not be built at all.

I implore you not to just read this book, but to take the actions and learning into your daily life. The best time is to start now. Take action. Any action is better than no action, as you cannot change the direction of a ship unless it is moving. Do it, dream, make mistakes, learn, change direction, congratulate yourself and succeed.

Harry O. Triguboff, AO
Founder and Managing Director, Meriton Apartments Pty Ltd.

INTRODUCTION

"Dreaming without action is wishful thinking."
Chris Christoff and many other people

80% of the population never sets goals and 70% that do set them, fail to achieve them.

Wow! If those are the statistics for goal setting, why bother with this book? Because I was one of those statistics until one day I figured out why and how not to be.

In this book, we will move away from some of the traditional ideas for setting goals and bring in new concepts. We will deal with both clear goals and discoverable (unclear) goals.

Your goals are your blueprint for life. This analogy is one of the reasons I chose this book's cover art and the fact that, as you will soon see, I have a passion for property development.

In preparation for setting and achieving goals, we will address the biggest factors for success and failure – what goes on inside your own head. We will address fear and procrastination by understanding why they occur and how to use them to your advantage. Many goals are not achieved because the person does not believe they deserve the outcome, so I will show you how to build belief and with it, the confidence to press on and achieve. We will deal with failure in a different way.

In order for a goal to be a driver for your actions you must see it as clearly as possible. Most texts use the term "visualize" to describe the process of seeing the goal in your head. For maximum effect, you will need to bring all of your senses into play. Firstly, because the more engagement you have with your goal, the more you are motivated to work towards it. Secondly, as each person has a different primary system for relating to the world, be it visual (seeing), auditory (sound), or kinesthetic (feeling), the goal should be thought about in those terms.

To encompass all of these modes I coined the term "Thinkualize." You will be thinking about what, in your mind, you can see, hear, taste, touch, smell and more, and what feelings and emotions your goal triggers in you. All of these components build a strong and compelling passion for the goal, the first step on the path to achievement.

Other goal setting methodologies drive timeframes hard. Timeframes for goal setting can be a contentious topic and can be a major factor for stress and eventual failure. We will address the question of timeframes differently to give you the best chance of achieving the outcome, by exploring approaches to timeframe setting dependent on the type of goal.

Sharing goals with others is a commonly advocated technique for keeping you accountable to your commitment to achieve the goal. There are times when a goal should be shared and times when it should not. When declaring a goal to others, it is important to understand with whom you should share it and when.

We will explore the need for mentors and show you how to go about getting a mentor. I will introduce you to the Nisi concept of self-mentorship.

There is a variety of other tools and techniques presented for use around the periphery of goal setting to help smooth the path to success.

Where I have developed beliefs about goal setting I have attempted to validate these against the works of others. This provides additional credibility so you can adopt these ideas with confidence. You will see references through the book that you can follow up for further information. Where possible, I have used material freely available on the Internet. Where publications and journals are referenced, you can get the results and conclusions freely by looking up the publication's abstract, although often a Google search will locate the full text article for you.

Much of this book is written in the first person (I said, I did, etc.) as I refer to my own experiences to show you that it can be done. I talk about my successes and failures, the way I think about things and the methods I use to achieve what I set out to do.

The key to achieving any goal, in spite of many of the notions of attraction only through visualization, is one thing – ACTION! At the end of most chapters, there are action statements for you to use. These are a summary of the actions, activities and processes discussed in the chapter.

Your next action is to read this book. Your next goal is to finish it. Have fun!

WHY I WROTE THIS BOOK

This book is a distillation of my experiences, learning and many years' experience in information technology, managing teams and projects. My experience and education have produced concepts, principles and practices that worked for me and through some diligent reimagining, will work for you. I also read some books that, well frankly, annoyed me to the point of wanting to say how it should be done. Another trigger for writing this book came after I left an 80 hour a week job to move into property investment and development. I achieved it in a way I did not envision.

I sat in many self-improvement seminars where the speaker championed the "secrets" of getting anything you could want. The common theme was that you have a dream, write your goals down, read them every day, set a time to achieve the goals and your goals will come to you.

My challenge was setting a timeframe based only on the outcome I wanted. Not only should I believe I can get what I want with no idea how, but I put added pressure on myself by insisting it be done by a certain date, or I set the date so far into the future it has no relevance. Have you experienced that? Did it work for you?

In managing big IT projects, you need to know the path to determine if the destination is possible, to decide whether the timeframe is realistic and what the costs are. You determine how long a project will take by knowing the steps required to get there and how long each takes. How is this any different from setting goals in life?

Well, it is different, but I am also correct, as YOU NEED *Goal (outcome)* + *Path (process)* to be successful, and the timeframe is dependent on the type of goal. The methods taught in the seminars I attended were incomplete. The goal and the path to get there are both equally important. The path is a series of actions, which in themselves are goals to be set and achieved. Seeing and feeling (yes, feeling) the goal with clarity will drive you to walk the path. Path setting and goal setting go together.

At the other extreme is the philosophy that you can sit and think about your goal and the universe will deliver it to you, like pizza. With my engineering education, I could not see how this could work[1]. All my life I was taught that I had to work for what I wanted. How could wishful thinking get it for me?

I believe in the power of visualization, of action and the power within you. Others believe in the power of the universe, including several of those accomplished people I interviewed, so you decide for yourself. In the end, it doesn't matter how you frame your motivations, as long as you are achieving goals.

If you are a sceptic, or a downright pragmatist, this book is for you. If you are not, this book is also for you. It will give you approaches to setting goals you can tailor to your beliefs, personality, motivation and success.

I hope my journey and experiences enhance yours.

---

1. I have a little play with the mathematics of transmission from the brain in The Last Chapter resource on the website.

THE PEOPLE I INTERVIEWED

> *"There's no such thing as can't."*
> Donna Campisi – Australian Speaker, Writer, Humanitarian, Crazy Runner
> and Adventurer, 1970-

I interviewed people from different professions and disciplines – property, finance, psychology, business, motor racing, pharmacy, business transformation, sales and marketing, return from adversity, farming, working people and on through to those with a psychic disposition. I chose pragmatists like me, who believe in science, logic and fact, through to successful people who use techniques like "the law of attraction" and "manifesting", to those driven by a calling to their religion. I wanted a large spectrum, a diversity of messages and styles, and to show that some themes are central to everybody's goal setting. I chose people who are everyday folk like you and me and who went on to great achievements through their goal setting.

There will be someone's story to which you can relate. Below are brief biographies of the interviewees. More information is available in the resources section of the website, including interview transcripts.

Throughout the book, there is PLY text relating the experience of these people. PLY means "People Like You" because that's what they are, ordinary folk like you, who set a goal and went for it, as you will.

Graham Bibby

Author, Speaker, Entrepreneur

As a kid Graham lived in government housing in England but came from a family with a strong work ethic. Graham was ridiculed at school, but was driven – he scrubbed floors, washed dishes, delivered milk in the dead of the English winter and worked with his dad on building sites. At age 21, Graham bought his first house and converted it to five apartments.

Graham had careers in the food and clothing industries, and in the finance industry in the UK and Asia. He was the former Chairman of the Technical Analyst Society of Hong Kong and the founding member of the Hong Kong Securities Institute.

Graham lives in Phuket, Thailand. Graham is the author of "*Master Your Mind, Master Your Money,*" with other books soon to be released.

Greatest Achievements:

- Various business ventures at a young age
- Formed a leading UK financial advisory company
- Formed Hong Kong and Asia premier asset management companies
- Built houses and a luxury 92 private-villa resort in Thailand
- Started The Insiders Club to guide ordinary investors

Donna Campisi

Speaker, Writer, Humanitarian, Crazy Runner and Adventurer

At the age of eight Donna had a stroke, which resulted in organ problems, loss of speech, and left her unable to move the right side of her body. Doctors told her she would never again walk. When she was 14, doctors diagnosed her with Type 1 Diabetes.

After training herself to walk as a child, in adult life Donna wanted to run again. In 11 months, she progressed from 30 steps to completing a marathon – 30,000 steps. Through her *Run Donna Run* events and adventures, Donna continually challenges herself and raises money for the hospital that saved her life (several times). Donna's story featured in her e-book *"Turn Dreams into Reality – 9 people who challenged themselves and ran with it!"* Donna is writing a book on her life story from stroke to marathon. Donna lives in Melbourne, Victoria, Australia.

Greatest Achievements – Living, talking, walking, running and building RunDonnaRun and all it represents.

Jacqui Christie

Psychologist, Therapist, Counsellor, Coach, Author, Speaker

Jacqui Christie, "The Intuitive Psychologist," is a registered Clinical and Counselling Psychologist. Jacqui's 22 years in psychology has seen her develop and implement programs addressing violence, anger, behavior, parenting, stress, mindfulness and depression. She is a relationship therapist and trained in clinical hypnosis.

As a child, Jacqui lived in three different countries as her father was in the Royal Air Force in England. None of her family had gone to university but both parents were especially hard working, a trait Jacqui inherited.

After careers in IT and retail, while a full time mother, Jacqui decided on a career change to fulfil her passion for helping people. Jacqui attended night school and then university. Ten years later, with undergraduate and graduate qualifications, Jacqui became a psychologist. Jacqui is also the author of the book *"Rewire your Relationship, A practical guide to creating a loving and passionate relationship."* Jacqui is married and lives in Melbourne, Victoria, Australia.

Greatest achievement – Becoming a psychologist and living her dream life helping people.

Julius Czerny

Business Owner, Franchisee, Elite Sportsman, Speaker, Author, Heart Attack Survivor

Competitive physical activity dominated Julius' life as a means of maintaining a healthy body, which benefited him in ways he never imagined. This fitness, friends who could help, and having life insurance stood him in good stead on the day he suffered a massive heart attack and lived to tell the tale. Julius relates his experience around the world, speaking to audiences on health and success. Julius is the author of the book *"Dead One Day, Laughing The Next – How CPR and Insurance Saved My Life and Tips That Can Save You Too."* Julius lives on the Gold Coast, Queensland, Australia, with his partner Helen.

Greatest achievements – Achieving his goals in sports and business and, because of his sports training, surviving a massive heart attack.

Patricia Dennis

Author, Poet, Painter, Entrepreneur, World Traveler

Patricia, as a seven year old, and her family, were forced by the Japanese to live in the Santo Tomas Concentration Camp in Manila during World War II. Patricia, as a young woman, gravitated towards catwalk and television fashion modelling, in Australia and overseas. Her tenacity and positivity have led Patricia into many business ventures including cattle farming, designing and manufacturing accessories for big Australian stores, designing women's fashion and jewelry, and developing real estate. Her book, *"Hell to Happiness – A Concentration Camp Childhood to a Life of Abundance,"* is a memoir of her magnificent and tumultuous life. Tricia, as family and friends know her, lives in Gippsland, Victoria, Australia.

Greatest achievement – Overcoming the horrors and adversities of being in a concentration camp as a child, to building many successful careers and businesses.

Tony Gattari

Entrepreneur, Business Strategy Coach, Property Developer

Tony grew up in outer western Sydney, Australia, to hard working Italian parents.

With a degree in business, Tony convinced Gerry Harvey of Harvey Norman Retail to give him a job. Tony eventually became General Manager of the computer division. Tony increased the division's turnover from $12 million to a staggering $565 million. Harvey Norman is now a large Australian-based retailer of electrical, computer, furniture and entertainment goods, with a presence in nine countries.

Tony's current business provides business and marketing strategy to large, medium and small business. Some of his large business clients include Cisco, Australia Post, Gloria Jeans, Harvey Norman, LG Electronics, Rebel Sport and more than 100 small to medium sized businesses.

Tony has established and run a successful technology company and has stepped into companies as CEO, Managing Director or Marketing Director to improve the company's position. Tony is also involved in property development. Tony knows that business is about people and has become a master at assessing people and motivating them to reach their potential. Tony lives in Sydney, New South Wales, Australia.

Greatest achievement – Taking the fledgling Harvey Norman computer store from a $12 million annual turnover to $565 million.

John Gearon

Executive Coach, Outcome Strategist

John is one of Australia's leading executive coaches and outcome strategists. Coming from a background as a dyslexic, unfit, overweight earthmoving equipment driver, John turned his life around to compete in 280 triathlons, 23 marathons and 15 Ironman championships, including World championships. John developed specialist knowledge in exercise physiology, human nutrition and behavioral psychology. People seek John's expertise in business, sport, leadership, organizational turn-around and business communication. John has worked with Anthony Robbins (USA Results Coach), John Gray of the Mars & Venus publishing empire, Steven Covey of Seven Habits fame and Tad James (NLP Educator). John has conducted peak performance training for the armed forces and for many sporting coaches. John features in the *"Mr. Millionaire"* and *"Health and Wellbeing Millionaire"* books by Fiona Jones et al. John lives with his wife, Jannine, on the Gold Coast, Queensland, Australia.

Greatest achievement – Transforming himself into to a successful outcomes strategist, whose business is coaching people to high performance.

Kawena Gordon

International Author, Clairvoyant, Speaker, Mentor

Kawena is 88 years young, a dynamo of energy and is inspiring and motivating through sharing her lifetime secrets. Kawena lived a normal life as a wife and mother and then at the age of 45 she learned to sing, performing for 22 years at venues all over the Gold Coast, Australia. Kawena learned about breath control and teaches it as a path to good health and high energy levels. It is the topic of her book *"Happiness Is Just a Breath Away – How to Achieve High energy, Confidence & Vitality."*

Kawena is a healer and a clairvoyant, starting in her early 50's, and was inducted into the Psychics Hall of Fame by the Australian Psychics Association in 2013. Kawena's greatest joy is teaching others how to find and develop their own passion and purpose in life. Kawena lives on the Gold Coast, Queensland, Australia.

Sharon Jurd

International Author, Speaker, Entrepreneur, Business Executive

Sharon is a highly respected international best-selling author as well as a seasoned business executive, entrepreneur, growth strategist and success coach. Sharon is qualified and recognized as a leading business coach, with licenses as a real estate agent, auctioneer and stock and station agent and holds a diploma in business and franchising.

Sharon has a passion for peak performance and creating success. Six months after she opened her first real estate franchise, she obtained a 72% market share. Within the year, Sharon had opened her second office – as the youngest female director in the organization. Sharon's success continued despite a debilitating illness taking her away from the business for a year.

Sharon is now the director of her own franchise network, HydroKleen Australia, the leader in its field. Sharon has 36 industry and business awards including Franchise Business of the Year, Chamber of Commerce Business of the Year, State Franchise Woman of the Year, and Australian Franchise Woman of the Year.

For more than 20 years Sharon has worked, travelled, consulted and taught internationally, speaking to and motivating thousands of people in nine countries on creating wealth and financial success.

She is the international author of the book, *"How To Grow Your Business Faster Than Your Competitor – The Secrets to Freedom and Success in 5 Easy Steps"* and her latest book is *"Extraordinary Women in Franchising – How their businesses have grown and how yours can too."*

Sharon lives on the Gold Coast, Queensland, Australia, with her partner John.

Greatest achievements – Building successful businesses and encouraging others to succeed.

Dr. X

Medical Doctor, Specialist

Dr. X's identity has been disguised for professional reasons. Having studied arts at school, Dr. X started as a medical assistant for a doctor. Encouraged by various mentors, Dr. X studied hard and entered medical school. Today, as a doctor with over 25 years' experience, Dr. X has a reputation for compassion and a dedication to improving the management of pain in patients.

Dr. X struggled with personal health issues for four years. As doctors couldn't do anything, Dr. X embarked on a voyage of discovery and found a cure. This experience shapes one's view of the world, bringing a deep understanding of being a patient in the medical system.

Dr. X is a sought-after pain specialist, speaker and author. By using imagery and visualization techniques, Dr. X helps patients needing medical care learn to cope with the demands of the modern healthcare system. Dr. X created innovative pain management workshops, conducted for patients requiring long-term hospital care. Dr. X presents successful case studies at national and international conferences and is an author.

Greatest achievements – Becoming a doctor and curing oneself of a four-year debilitating illness.

Tiffany Mason

Motivational Speaker, Author and Personal Development Coach

Tiffany turned her life around after being subjected to abuse, which destroyed a promising international skating career. Tiffany is the author of "*The Power of Adversity: A Guide To Finding Your Greatest Gift In Life*," and Founder of Mason Coaching and Consulting, LLC – an education and coaching company working with professional women who experience exhaustion and disconnection within their personal life. Tiffany helps professional women design a successful career, while establishing a meaningful personal life at home. Tiffany's moto is, "*Be the change you want to be. Design the life you want to experience.*" Tiffany lives in West Point, New York, with her husband, John.

Greatest Achievement – Forgiving the man who subjected her to abuse and, from adversity, building a career in helping women through their own adversities.

Paul Moni

Owner, Moni Solutions Pty Ltd and Financial Services Consultant

Paul has had an illustrious career in the world of business and finance. Here is a short list of accomplishments:

- 23 years with international accounting firms in Australia and the United Kingdom
- Seven years with Australian Securities and Investments Commission
- Over 20 years with major international marketing and advertising agencies in Australia and the USA
- Consulting in USA and Australia, to private enterprise and government
- University Adjunct Professor, University of Queensland
- National President – Chartered Secretaries Australia
- Independent Director – Large private companies
- Technical Adviser to The Institute of Chartered Accountants in Australia

Paul and his wife, Barbara, live in Brisbane, Queensland, Australia.

Greatest Achievement – Appointed National President of the Governance Institute of Australia, a member-based organization representing governance and risk professionals in Australia. Paul selected this achievement as he had to solve a large range of complex issues.

Darren Morgan

Top Fuel Racing Team Owner and Driver

Darren, Morgs to his friends, has hurtled down a racetrack at 300mph (482kph), reaching those speeds in four seconds. Darren drove for, and managed, racing teams before starting his own in 2007. Darren is the owner and manager of Australia's most successful Top Fuel motor racing team.

The team has taken out three consecutive Top Fuel Championships (2011, 2012 and 2013). With his 2005 win, Darren is the only person ever to win four championships. His handpicked team outperforms teams with more experience, manpower and funds. The team is a family business with wife Natalie and kids Caitlyn and Rory.

When Darren is not racing, he is teaching motorsport at his local college. Motor racing is an expensive sport, so Darren does shows, teaches people to drive and whatever it takes to raise the funds to pursue his passion. Darren, Natalie and their family, live in Mildura, Victoria, Australia.

Greatest achievements – His amazing family and his world class Top Fuel racing team.

Joanne Verikios

Health Industry Entrepreneur, Horse Breeder, Trainer and Judge, Athlete, Real Estate Investor, and an accomplished Author.

Joanne received her first pony at the age of nine, after years of negotiation with her parents (yes, negotiation). She earned the qualification of Instructor at age sixteen and saw success as a member of the team winning the Duke of Edinburgh Pony Club Games Championship in 1972.

Joanne progressed to training and racing thoroughbreds and founding and managing the Highborn Warmblood Stud. In recognition of her 30-year contribution to the Australian Warmblood Horse Association, Joanne achieved Honorary Life Membership in 2015. Joanne is a past Federal President and Federal Registrar of the Association, which she continues to serve.

Joanne was also an Australian Powerlifting Champion, holding State, National and Commonwealth records. Twice, Joanne represented Australia at the Women's World Powerlifting Championships. Joanne accomplished all of this while working as a Senior Executive for the Australian Public Service for 32 years.

Joanne has published articles in many equine publications. Her latest book is *"Winning Horsemanship – A Judge's Secrets and Tips for Your Success."* Joanne and her husband, George, live in Brisbane, Queensland, Australia.

Greatest achievement – Nine years of pestering, cajoling and strategic maneuvering to get her first pony, such was her passion for horses.

Coral Brian-Wheatley

Real Estate Investor, Entrepreneur, Chef, Restaurateur and Teacher

Coral is a self-made multi-millionaire, successful real estate investor of more than 30 years, entrepreneur, celebrated chef and experienced restaurateur. She purchased her first investment property at 16.

After retiring at the age of 35, Coral and her husband Ron continue to build their multimillion-dollar real estate empire. Their real estate portfolio includes homes, apartments, townhouses, caravan parks, motels, storage bays, work bays, and shopping centers. Coral is a self-taught share trader and investor, growing her self-managed super fund[2] for more than 17 years. Coral is the author of *"Building Wealth in a Self-Managed Super Fund – How I Turned $80k into $4million and How You Can Too."* Coral and Ron live in Coffs Harbour, New South Wales, Australia.

Greatest achievements – Ability to pick out a property bargain, solve problems and build an extensive portfolio of commercial and residential property.

2. Superannuation (called Super) is a pension fund, paid into by both employer and employee, similar to a US 401(k). In Australia, the beneficiaries can manage the investment of these funds.

Gai Williams

International Author, Entrepreneur, Businesswoman and Leading Pharmacist

Gai Williams is a woman of many firsts. Gai's first job was in a pharmacy at fourteen years of age. Gai bought her first pharmacy in 1992, a time when banks wouldn't lend money to young women with children, in partnership with a friend's husband whom she credits as a mentor. Gai started Pharm-A-Temp in 1997, Victoria's first independent fee-for-service pharmacy locum business, still in operation today. She twice refitted her pharmacy, the flagship concept store for Guardian Pharmacies Australia, one of the Australia's most trusted brands with over 200 stores nationally.

Gai has watched the industry change with competition from supermarket chains and increased government regulation and has seen many other pharmacies disappear. Gai was elected as the first-ever female Chair of the Board of Guardian Pharmacies Australia.

After 18 months of negotiations, Gai convinced the premier international coffee brand, Gloria Jean's Coffees, to locate one of its franchises in her pharmacy. This was the first in Australia.

Gai has taken on the reins of the production and sale of a colic relief mixture for infants. Through a product developed by an Australian pharmacist, Gai has developed a market niche in treating baby colic in Australia and overseas with the No More Tears Colic Relief program. Gai is the international author of the book, *"No More Tears – Colic Relief."* Gai is a lifelong Essendon (Bombers) AFL football fan and she and her husband live in Melbourne, Victoria, Australia.

Greatest achievement – Going into business for herself in a time when women were not supported in business, then prospering and making a difference to people's lives.

CHAPTER
1

What is goal setting?

You do it every day

CHAPTER 1

What is goal setting? You do it every day

> *"You are never too old to set another goal or to dream a new dream."*
> C. S. Lewis – British Novelist, Poet, Academic, 1898-1963

> *"Goal setting is not a mechanical process. It is training your subconscious to enjoy defining and achieving goals."*
> Chris Christoff

> *"Make your goals addictive."*
> Marc Miles – Australian Educator, Trainer, Speaker, Entrepreneur, 1979-

Let's get something clear from the start. You are a goal setter and goal achiever!

Every day you set goals to get to work or school, to work through the day's activities and meet your work or school deadlines. You set reminders to awake in the morning and for family and friends' birthdays. You put wedding invitations on the fridge, along with pictures of your next holiday destination. You plan weekend adventures. You arrange other transport if your car is in for repairs or if there is a public transport breakdown. You ask others for help or advice.

You plan ahead, tackle the small goals, schedule timeframes, meet deadlines, put up reminders and display motivating images, overcome obstructions and seek mentorship. You do all of the little actions that navigate you to the bigger goals – each day, each year, life.

You are a goal setter!

Admittedly, some of those examples are more like tasks than goals but the principle is the same. You identify what you want or need, you plan a path to get it, you take the actions, engage others to help when needed and you reach the goal.

Goal achievement is the systematic performance of the required steps to reach a target, something you want. Goal setting is often taught as a "mechanical" process that takes discipline and willpower. I believe there needs to be flexibility, even tailoring the process to your personality, for everything from defining the goal to working out the path and setting the timeframe, to how you adjust for obstacles, setbacks and even failures. This philosophy drives the methods in this book.

In his book, "*Psycho-Cybernetics*," first published in 1960 and modernized in 2001[i], Maxwell Maltz, a cosmetic surgeon, tells how many of his patients suffered from poor self-esteem and through his practice he helped correct that, rather than use the surgeon's knife. His book discusses the principles of modern goal setting and self-improvement, including visualization, affirmations and the workings of the subconscious as an automatic success mechanism. He likens our success instinct to a missile wandering off course, using this feedback to correct the error and reset the course back on track to the target. The missile drifts off-target, corrects and then drifts off again. The missile literally fails its way to the target. Maltz's automatic success system is your subconscious and Reticular Activating System (RAS).

Reticular Activating System

The RAS is an intricate collection of neuron circuits connecting the brainstem (the movement and sensory part) to the cortex (the thinking part) of the brain. Primarily it controls wakefulness, attention and the sleep-wake transitions.

The RAS is a filter, controlling the information getting to your brain and hence, what you pay attention to. The RAS plays a part in your survival instincts by bringing to your attention anything threatening you. Your attention is quickly focused, for example, by loud noises, if you think you see a snake or when you hear your name spoken across a noisy room. Your fight-or-flight mechanism activates if there is danger, preparing your body to run or to fight. It fires off adrenaline, dopamine and serotonin to ready your muscles and your brain for fast action. It increases heart rate and blood flow, dilates pupils of the eyes to see better, and increases blood sugar level for the energy you may need for intense physical activity.

The RAS, able to process 100 million signals per second, has a pre-conscious awareness of the environment and feeds information to your conscious mind for decision and action. The RAS provides needed information based on what your conscious mind is doing. If you are looking for something, you provide a picture of it to your RAS and it helps to "notice" it. This is also why sometimes you can't find it when it is in plain sight because you have the wrong picture (which results in conversations like this with my wife – "Chris, it is right there in front of you!" "No it's not…oh, yes it is…I thought it was blue not red").

The RAS is the "noticer," picking up on the unusual or changes, things new or different, in the environment and signaling them as is necessary to the conscious. The RAS and associated brain systems are your autopilot. When you decide to do something, the RAS and the subconscious go to work guiding you to achieve it. Often it is without conscious thought, leaving you to think about something else. As simple examples, consider these – driving to work and not noticing how many red lights there were, or knitting a sweater while watching TV and carrying on a conversation. One key element here is, through practice, repetition and experience, those people are able to perform those activities with considerable skill and their subconscious guides them now. They trained their subconscious minds.

If someone points something out to you that you didn't notice before, your RAS will notice those things in the environment. Have you experienced the situation where you bought a new car/clothing/jewelry and then noticed lots of other people with the same thing? After a while, you stop noticing as it is no longer novel. The RAS helps you seek out what you want and helps look for opportunities, and solutions to obstacles. Sounds perfect for goal achievement, if you program it, doesn't it?

Performing the actions required to deliver the outcomes, assisted by the deliberate training of the subconscious, is the path to goal achievement. You train the subconscious through affirmations, visualizations (thinkualizations) and the feedback from performing the actions and succeeding or failing. Thinkualization is a big part and we will explore this deeply, as it is far more than just a picture in the mind.

Visionary people set goals

History is replete with pioneers, entrepreneurs, adventurers, athletes, activists and leaders who dared to believe in a possibility that had not previously existed – Albert Einstein, Christopher Columbus, Roger Bannister, Rosa Parks and Nelson Mandela, to name but a few. These people believed in a dream that did not exist before they set their sights on their goal. In a real way, they created their own reality and in so doing, changed the world forever.

What we believe is possible *absolutely* determines our reality. On May 6th 1954, Roger Bannister ran a mile in 3 minutes 59.4 seconds – the first time four minutes had been broken since accurate recordings started back in 1850. For 104 years, everyone thought that breaking this four minute milestone was outside the capabilities of the human body. It only took 46 days before someone else, John Landy, an Australian, broke Bannister's record. By the end of 1957, 16 runners had broken the magic four minute mile. Why? The psychological barriers lifted due to evidence.

> **"Whether you believe you can do a thing or not –**
> **you are right!"**
> Henry Ford – American Industrialist,
> Founder of the Ford Motor Company, 1863-1947

Goal setting and goal achievement does require some preparation. It requires a goal and there are ways for you to determine what your goals could be. A belief that you can have what you are aiming for, and that you do deserve the reward at the end of the path, are required. Goal setting will put pressure on you, so tools are required to deal with stress and procrastination and for getting around or through obstacles on the path. We will work through the process step-by-step and the next chapter, on deserving, will launch you on the path.

CHAPTER
2

Deserving your Dreams, Success is a Mindset

CHAPTER 2

Deserving your Dreams, Success is a Mindset

"The minute you settle for less than you deserve, you get even less than you settled for."
Maureen Dowd – American Columnist, Author, Pulitzer Prize Winner, 1952-

"The mindset engendered by responsibility without guilt is the platform for knowing you deserve. Knowing!"
Chris Christoff

Before we get into defining and setting goals, some preparatory work is required to set the stage to achieve maximum success. In the next few chapters, we will explore deserving, handling stresses and fears limiting goal achievement and, a powerful tool in goal achievement, your subconscious.

To achieve any goal you must first feel you deserve it, otherwise it is likely you will not achieve it or, if you do, you will not hold on to it. The feeling you don't deserve an outcome can be an obstacle to setting and achieving goals. It leads to self-sabotage by thought and action resulting in perceived failure reinforcing the feeling of not deserving (self-fulfilling destructive cycle).

PLY: To deserve you have to allow others to deserve.
John – "People see an expensive car pull up outside a fancy restaurant. The unenlightened might say, 'Well, look at that show off. He is probably a drug dealer.' The enlightened might say, 'Well look at that, I wonder what he does for a living to be so successful. I wonder if I could do that.'"

The word "deserve" is derived from the Latin word "deservire," meaning, "To serve well." The meaning gradually shifted to that of "to earn or be entitled to by serving well." To DEserve you need to RE-serve, not Reserve. You deserve the goal by doing everything needed to reach the goal, taking the required actions and doing it for as long as it takes. If you are reserved, shy or unwilling, then it is likely you won't reach the goal, which will feel undeserved. Building your skills and confidence enables you to serve yourself well and to deserve what you want from life.

Deserving is about being confident in what you want from life. Build this confidence through steps on the way to the goal. The first step is clarity, to have a clear idea of what it is you want and why you want it and how you will get it. The more you work on the clarity, the "what, why and how," the more certainty you feel. As you set the path and work to get to the goal, your feelings of certainty strengthen. As certainty develops, the power in the feeling of knowing where you are going builds confidence. As confidence grows, you make decisions and take actions with more courage – The Clarity, Certainty, Confidence, Courage[3] cycle.

PLY: *Coral remembers many negative people around in the early days, warning her off buying property. She and her husband followed strict criteria for evaluating a property. This gave them certainty, and with that, the confidence to successfully invest and the courage to take calculated risks.*

You will hear many speakers and authors, from many of life's activities that seek some type of mastery, refer to one or more of these principles in the pursuit of success. The process of developing each of the C's runs in parallel with the others. As each is grown a little, they in turn grow the others. You don't need to have them all, or any of them, to be bullet-proof to start with. Wealthy people, whether wealthy in finance, relationships, career or any other of life's endeavors, act in the face of fear and do not run.

PLY: *Dr X had to re-sit a chemistry exam while studying to be a doctor and got an A on the exam – "I think it gave me more confidence. I was quite chuffed ... It did help. Just knowing I could. If I applied myself, I could do things." Dr X sailed through the final exams.*

---

3. Strangely, the first reference I can find bringing these principles together is from the Prussian General and Military Theorist, Carl von Clausewitz (1780 – 1831). He is most famous for his military treatise "Vom Kriege", translated into English as "On War", a book in every strategist's library.

> *"Confidence isn't optimism or pessimism and it's not a character attribute. It's the expectation of a positive outcome."*
> Rosabeth Moss Kanter – Professor, Harvard University, 1943-

Responsibility

> *"It is easy to dodge our responsibilities but we cannot dodge the consequences of dodging our responsibilities."*
> Sir Josiah Stamp – English Industrialist, Economist, Statistician, Writer and Banker, 1881-1941

One of the key traits for accepting that you deserve what you want is taking responsibility, responsibility without guilt. Taking responsibility feeds into the confidence and courage parts of the CCCC cycle.

You must take responsibility for everything in your life. Everything, whatever has happened and will happen to you, is your responsibility. You were responsible for yourself from the minute you were born. You told your parents you were hungry, hot, cold or in pain. Whether or not you cause everything that happens to you, you choosing to believe that you are responsible for all that happens to you is empowering. You are responsible through agency (an action you intended to do) and through negligence (ignoring the situation and letting it develop). Making the choice gives you control, taking you from victim to victor, giving you power to make changes to get results.

However, accepting that everything is your responsibility does not mean it is your fault. Whatever happens, even if it is not your fault, you take responsibility. If something has been inflicted on you, such as accident or illness, you take responsibility for your recovery. Having a "woe is me" attitude will not fix the problem. Take responsibility for your actions and encourage yourself to address any issues, and then move on. This is a positive outcome for you and hopefully others around you (except for those wishing to live life in the negative and keep you there with them). The solution may be to do nothing and accept the situation. If that is your decision, do so and move on.

In accepting responsibility, you do not take on any guilt. The natural process in a healthy organism is for wounds to close up and heal. If you keep opening the wound it will not heal, it will fester and it will affect your wellbeing. Guilt is the equivalent of opening the wound and reopening it every time you revisit the guilt.

> *"Responsibility is a driver, guilt is an anchor."*
> Chris Christoff

Guilt anchors you in the past, a past that you cannot change. Guilt prevents you from healing yourself and healing relationships and moving forward. Whatever happens, you take responsibility for your actions and your feelings and you learn from the experience. Responsibility is a driver, guilt is an anchor.

There are some philosophies where guilt is a central tenet, a method of control of the populace, control of thinking and attitude. You are better off, whatever your belief system, purging yourself of this guilt. Can you change what happened? No. Review the situation, make amends where necessary, learn any lessons from it, then drop it and move on. Care for the wound, dress it, medicate it, let it heal, learn from the experience and forget about it. This is responsibility.

While you take responsibility without guilt, you still feel and express empathy and sympathy. You are not a cold-hearted sociopath (if you are, you probably don't need to read this chapter). When something you did contributed to the problem, feel and express those emotions and take responsibility, rectify the situation and move on. If you let the guilt become debilitating and if you permit (yes, permit) others to drag you back into it, you are not able to do the best you can for them or yourself. As the inflight spiel goes "Put on your own mask before helping others."

Taking responsibility for everything that happens to you enables and encourages you to step up, to be confident and brave. It establishes a mindset that reduces dependence on others and their influence. I remind my wife when she raises some past mistake on my part (do all wives do that?) that I cannot change the past, I have lived it, learned from it and moved on.

Now, having acknowledged your responsibility, should you do everything yourself, alone? No, of course not. You are assisted by the actions of others, but you take responsibility for choosing them and instructing them if they are providing a service to you (e.g., your staff) or for determining their needs and requirements if you are delivering a service for them (e.g., your management or customers). If someone is not delivering what is required, you take action, communicate, provide clarity and training or, if the situation deserves it, you fire them (whether staff or customer).

PLY: *John – "People have to participate in their own rescue. Take ownership, accountability and responsibility for your actions and don't live in blame, excuses or denial. Achievement requires the pain of sacrifice, which is a far better pain than that resulting from woulda-shoulda-coulda."*

Taking responsibility encourages you to plan, as you know you are responsible. Thinkualizing the outcomes you require and pursuing them can only be successful if you are responsible otherwise you are just wishing and hoping. Hope means maybe, maybe not. Expectation means you expect it. Responsibility drives expectation.

Why are we talking about responsibility in the context of deserving? The mindset engendered by responsibility without guilt is the platform for knowing that you deserve. It is your responsibility if you don't get the outcome and if you do. The strength of mind that comes with taking responsibility, with the expectation of the result, a result thinkualized in detail, enables you to accept the outcome when it arrives. There is no question of "do I deserve this?" as you will have it because you planned it, built it, you took the path and took the actions to deliver the outcome. You deserve it.

Developing a strong platform for building and achieving your goals will sustain you when you achieve them, so you get to keep them. There is no perfect way, or even right way, to set and achieve goals. In this book, you will find information for you to develop your own way. When you get there and think about how you did it, you don't need to have waged some sort of precision tactical "campaign" to achieve the goal. It is quite OK for you to be unsure along the way, about both the goal itself and the path. As you progress, these will be defined and refined. It is OK for the goal to change because, as you gain more clarity about what you want and a better understanding of yourself, you craft the original idea into the final goal. It is OK for you to change direction and take multiple paths to the goal, sometimes having to backtrack. This is all part of you letting yourself succeed.

Taking responsibility and growing your CCCC may also help reduce an effect called Imposter Syndrome. From Wikipedia, "Impostor Syndrome" is a psychological phenomenon in which people are unable to internalize their accomplishments. *"Despite external evidence of their competence, those with the syndrome remain convinced that they are frauds and do not deserve the success they have achieved."*[ii] In their publication, Clance and Imes discuss the imposter phenomenon predominantly affecting high achieving women.[iii]

> **"Our deepest fear is not that we are inadequate.**
> **Our deepest fear is that we are powerful beyond measure."**
> Marianne Williamson – American Poet, Author, Lecturer, 1952-

Some famous people have publicly stated feelings of not deserving their success – Academy Award winners Jodie Foster and Kate Winslett, producer of the Batman movies Michael Uslan and others.[iv] These people have achieved greatness. Give yourself the opportunity to do the same. When you value yourself, the world values you. When you have something to contribute to the world and you value it, the world will value it.

The Reason Why

There is a key element assisting in defining clarity, developing goal ownership and understanding the underlying motivation for wanting it – it is the reason why.

PLY: *Graham's "why" stems from his childhood and drove his success – "A passion to get out of being ridiculed. I was beaten up most days on the way to school as we lived in an area normally reserved for ex criminals. I was regularly tormented at school by teachers."*

Coral's "why" came from the workload of owning her own restaurant – "That was more or less seven days a week, 12 to 14 hours a day and I knew that I wasn't capable of keeping that up ... I wanted to be financially independent." And what is her deep down reason? "I think it might have been a little bit of fear, of not being in control."

In understanding the reason why, you will better understand and accept why you deserve it. In going through this exercise, you take the key desire from the subconscious to the conscious, bringing it into the open for scrutiny. When you understand it, you can tailor the definition of the goal and the thinkualization to resonate directly with the desire.

For the reason why to motivate you, you must be true to yourself. You may think the core reason is not "unselfish" enough or not "grandiose" enough, so you ignore it and let it subconsciously hold you back (self-sabotage). Bringing it to the conscious helps you to own and accept it and you are able to acknowledge and use it. It is your reason and no one else's. Don't reveal it to anyone else, keep it to yourself. Mikaela Shiffrin, world ski champion, says *"I have many goals, but I don't talk about all of them to everyone. Some might seem too lofty, arrogant, or downright crazy to other people."*

Finding the reason why is simple to do. Keep asking yourself why, why, why? For each answer you give, ask why again. Ask, "Why am I doing this?" Pretend another person is asking you why and is not satisfied with your answer, so they keep asking.

PLY: *Joanne on asking "why? why?" – "The first answer usually isn't it. You've got to dig down to 'what will that give you?' And 'what will that give you?' And 'what will that look like and how does that feel?'"*

Alternatively, imagine you have already achieved the goal.

- What has this goal done for me?

- How has it made my life better?

- What has it done for my family, friends, colleagues?

- What would life be like if I had not achieved the goal?

- How will my life be different one week or one year after completing the goal?

- What can I now do that I couldn't do before?

- What opportunities have opened up for me?

PLY: *Donna had several reasons why she trained and ran a marathon – for herself to develop physically, because people said she couldn't, to raise funds for the hospital, for the memory of her brother and ultimately, so that she didn't let down the people who mentored her or who supported her fund raising. Even though there were benefits to others, all of these "whys" reward Donna.*

The idea is for you to get to your core motivations and key benefits for wanting the goal. Let's look at a hypothetical example:

Let's suppose Liam wants to set a goal to save money and buy a new car.

He asks himself, "Why do I want a new car?" Answer: "My wife wants me to get one."

This is her wish, not Liam's so he asks again, why? – "The radio doesn't work, the air conditioning is intermittent."

He asks again, why? – "My current car is old and unreliable and has broken down at times."

He asks again, why? – "I want to transport family and friends safely."

Why? – "I am embarrassed in front of my friends and I am tired of making excuses for it."

Why? – "I want my clients to have a good impression of me as a successful person."

He could continue and dig further.

As Liam digs deeper and answers honestly, he uncovers some deeply powerful emotions to form a vision of the goal that will motivate him to strive for it. He wants to feel proud of himself, wants the outward trappings of success, wants reliable transport, to ensure he and his passengers are safe and wants to be proud to share his car. Are these altruistic or grandiose reasons? It doesn't matter because they are real and they are his. He deserves to have his family transported safely, his friends to be comfortable and his clients to have a good impression. He doesn't need to tell anyone else what his reasons are. If he accepts them, they can drive him to the goal so he and others reap the benefits.

PLY: *Donna – "I would be struggling at times and asking myself, 'Why am I doing this?' … Of course, I have a number of reasons. My "whys," that's what kept me going, that was my drive".*

Jacqui had careers in retail and IT before finding one that satisfied her why – helping people.

Darren – "Why? Because we could. We wanted to be the best. I want the best team, the best crew, the best looking race car, the best looking crew, the crew having the most fun, the whole picture."

In *Chapter 9 – Constructing Your Goals*, we will look at how to construct and write goals and how to use these powerful reasons.

Expectation

> **"Responsibility drives expectation."**
> Chris Christoff

Cultivating expectation is the next step in deserving. Expectation is like pretending you will get what you want. Kim Gordon, American musician, said, *"It's amazing how many things you can do when you're just pretending."*

After I completed a contract working 80-hour weeks for a year, I took some time off and renovated two houses. After the break, I looked for a new IT role while preparing to make a living from property. I applied for the role as IT project manager for the G20, a meeting of the world leaders and central bank governors from 20 major economies (including USA, Australia, European Union and countries from South America and Asia). I went into the interviews expecting to get the job and came out with the same expectation. I have done this several times in the past.

These expectations came from thinkualizing and imagining the roles. I visualized what was required of the role and linked this to my previous experiences. I thinkualized how I would approach the required duties, how I would behave in the interview and how I would respond to the selection criteria. The roles were mine, I wanted them and the organizations offered them to me. Why? – Clarity, certainty, confidence, courage.

Expectation is a key enabler to meet your goals. It is not hope, hope is a case of "Maybe it will work, maybe it won't." Proceed as if you expect the outcome you want. Expectation will tell your subconscious how to work for you. Your attitude, tone of voice, bearing and reactions will convey your expectations to others. Your body language will tell others you mean what you say and know what you want.

> *"High achievement always takes place in the*
> *framework of high expectation."*
> Charles Kettering – American Inventor, Engineer, Businessman
> and the Holder of 186 Patents, 1876-1958

When you ask[4] others for something and expect to receive it, your demeanor and confidence convey a subconscious message, increasing the likelihood of compliance with your wishes. When someone tells you "no," a response contrary to your expectations, your reaction will convey a message of determination, which will in turn influence the interaction.

Expect encounters with others to go well. The secret to this is in knowing what "going well" means and knowing what you want from the encounter, which in turn comes from thinkualizing the outcome. Rehearse in your mind how you want the interaction to go, what the objections could be and how you will deal with them. This provides more certainty, generating the confidence to expect.

Plan like you expect, take action as if you expect, sell your ideas like you expect, ask as if you expect. When you order in a restaurant, you expect the waiter to place that dish in front of you. Use the same mindset and attitude when you ask for other things. The next time you go to a hotel in off-peak, test it by asking for a room upgrade. Prepare the ground first by thinking about and clearing the objections. For example, ask if the hotel has been busy. If not, there will be rooms available. Ask for the upgrade.

To modify the Paris 1968 slogan, "Be Practical, Expect the Impossible."

A Preparation Experience

Preparation is another tool for reinforcing what you want and what you deserve. Preparation may well be the path you take where the goal cannot be well defined or the timeframe cannot be readily predicted. To illustrate, let me tell you about my preparation for property development.

4. For more about Asking – see *The Last Chapter* resource on the website.

My goal was to leave IT and pursue property development and investment. Some of my "whys" included the need to create something tangible like "bricks and mortar," the feeling of financial security in property, knowing I built something real and profitable, something I could do almost anywhere in the world. High on the list of "whys" is to leave a legacy for my children, not only property and money but the knowledge and experience to do what I did. I want them along for the ride but I don't want to jeopardize their advancement with unnecessary risks. For this, I needed to get ready.

There are many ways to earn money from property. What could I do? Could I run my own property business? Preparation was necessary for me to understand if I could and to work out what the path was to a comparatively undefined goal.

PLY: *Julius on being prepared – "a lot of people say, 'You're lucky that you had three surf lifesavers'. I say, that's not luck. I chose that. For the past 45 years, I've been involved with those people. They say, 'You're lucky you're only in hospital for three days.' Again, that's not luck. I look after myself and I maintain my body. They say, 'You're lucky to get the six hundred percent return on your investment.' I say, again, that's not lucky, you could get it too, all you have to do is pay your high premiums and then die."*

How did I get ready? I focused on my passion. I visualized, as best I could, what I wanted to do and the rewards I wanted from the endeavor. I learned what I could through free and paid courses. I read everything I could find: books, blogs, emailing lists from property groups, magazines and the city/county council documents on others' developments. I went to realtor's open houses and attended auctions to observe. I spoke to professionals such as realtors, town planners and architects. I set goals to buy, renovate and sell a few houses. I made some mistakes and I had some successes. I also worked my way through a few mentors during the period. I contacted "experts" I thought might teach me something.

I had been to a presentation a year earlier when a particular developer was raising funds for a new venture. When I was ready, they appeared on the scene again. We talked about what I had done and what they had done. We talked about their new project and I proposed to invest in it but I had a caveat – I was along for the ride. The developers were happy to have me as a participant, not because of the money invested (they had many loyal backers to choose from) but because I was ready.

I am now involved in a multi-story, multi-million dollar residential property development in Brisbane, Australia. I get to go to the meetings with the architects, town planners and the local council. I get to study the reports from the engineers, soil technicians, acoustic engineers, town planners and traffic engineers. You may think this is boring but to me this is bliss, this is how I expand my knowledge in a real world case study. This is my apprenticeship to pursue my passion as fast as I can. How many other investors are along for the ride with me? None, either because they are not interested or they are not ready.

Because I focused, opportunities arose out of nowhere. Most importantly, I met my property mentors. Their teaching and encouragement, and the renovations I did, led to property magazine articles, radio interviews and webinars. I also did some teaching at seminars and on mentors' programs. Opportunities came from *know-where*.

Having a clear focus on what you want helps you to see the path, to the goal, when it appears because you are looking for it. Make the decision to go out rather than sit on the couch – you may meet the people with the opportunity or the person that will introduce them to you. You know what you want, so every decision you make aligns with you meeting that goal. You condition your mind so it knows. When you make a decision, what you really want influences your choice.

> **"The path to success is paved with opportunities.
> Your job is to see them."**
> Chris Christoff

I am still looking, learning, thinkualizing and dreaming because I have a long way to go to be where I want to be.

Action Statements

1. Exercise to remove guilt – Review the situation, make amends where necessary, learn any lessons from it, then drop it and move on.

2. Take responsibility, whatever happens, even if a negative outcome is not your fault.

3. Reasons – Ask yourself why, why, why? Dig deeper to find the true emotional drivers.

4. Plan like you expect, take action as if you expect, sell your ideas like you expect, ask as if you expect.

5. Prepare – It may well be that the path you take is where the goal cannot be well defined or the timeframe cannot be readily predicted.

CHAPTER
3

Managing Fear
and Stress

CHAPTER 3

Managing Fear and Stress

> **"Fears are educated into us and can, if we wish, be educated out."**
> Karl Augustus Menninger – American Practitioner and Advocate of Psychiatry, 1893-1990

> **"Emotions are the signals from your subconscious and they can be read."**
> Chris Christoff

Goal setting can be hard. People avoid it because they are afraid they will fail. They may also be afraid they will succeed, afraid of having a great life, not feeling they deserve it or that they can manage the responsibility that comes with being in control of their life. Harshly or poorly defined goals and timeframes induce stress, causing procrastination, which eventually results in failure to achieve the goal. You can manage these challenges and even use them to your advantage. Remember, challenges are not *in* the way, they are *on* the way to any goal.

Let's set the scene for you in terms of failure:

J.K Rowling, the author of Harry Potter – Divorced, raising a child, penniless, rejected by 12 publishers and told to get a day job as there was "no money in children's books." Her net worth is over $1 billion.

Nick Woodman – First two companies failed, lost $4 million, went on to invent the GoPro camera, now worth $2.6 billion.

Colonel Harland Sanders – Aged 66, almost broke, living off social security. Legend has it he had over 1,000 attempts to sell the first KFC franchise.

Walt Disney – Studio went bankrupt, created Disneyland after five years planning and much difficulty obtaining funding (purportedly over 300 banks refused).

James Dyson – 5,217 attempts over 15 years at inventing the bagless vacuum cleaner. Now worth $5 billion.

John Grisham – First book took three years to write and received rejection from 28 publishers.

Stephen King – First book was rejected 30 times.

Steve Jobs – Made some monumental mistakes including the Lisa, Apple III and PowerCube computers, hiring John Sculley as CEO who eventually sacked Jobs from Apple, Apple TV, NeXT computer, seeing Pixar as a hardware company. He tried to sell Pixar many times for $50m to break even and failed (luckily, as he eventually sold it to Disney for $7.4 billion). Pixar did many animated movies including Toy Story and Finding Nemo.

Michael Jordan – *"I have missed more than 9,000 shots in my career. I have lost almost 300 games. On 26 occasions, I have been entrusted to take the game winning shot, and I missed. I have failed over and over and over again in my life. And that is why I succeed."*

Richard Branson – Almost jailed for tax evasion with Virgin records, failures of Virgin Cola, Virgin Vodka, Virgin Brides, Virgin Ware, Virgin Clothing, Virgin Vie cosmetics, Virgin Cars, Virgin Digital, Virgin Pulse and Virgin Megastores. Branson is now worth $5.1 billion.

Henry Ford – Was broke five times before establishing the successful Ford Motor Company.

PLY – *Did they ever fail? Yes, here are a few examples...*

John – *Lost money and friendships through not doing due diligence on friends before getting into business.*

Coral – *Listened to people who said not to invest in Darwin, Australia, and the next year there was a huge property boom there. Also, she bought some poorly performing restaurants in shopping centres, going against her gut instinct.*

Gai – *Experimenting with strategies in her business* – *"Well, that honestly didn't work. We've spent enough money on it. We just stop it and we move on to something else."*

Donna – *"I have fallen so many times ...I would be struggling at times and asking myself, 'Why am I doing this?' ... I'm three-quarters of the way through my book ... It's not really failures as such, I think it's something that I haven't completed yet ... [Failure] It's a scary word."*

Jacqui – *"Essentially, the thing that went wrong or the failure, oh and I even hate to say that word. Oh! I can really feel it. The failure was in a business decision ... In being so generous and allowing everyone to do what they wanted, they took advantage of that."*

Paul – *A business Paul was involved in took on development of a software product (not core business). "The project plan was flawed at the start – the project manager did not have the skills to either understand or manage the project. ...[People] must have the required skills and experience."*

Tony – *"I wanted to become a CEO of a publicly listed company. I achieved that goal and it was horrible. It was a train wreck of the company. Once I had achieved that goal, I actually realized 'What am I doing here? I have no passion for this business.' I was actually not focused on what I consider to be my God-given gifts."*

Joanne *had many challenges with a property renovation project* – *"The failure was, I should have pulled the pin on it and just said, OK, I'm not going ahead with that, and put it on the market as it is... But I kind of hung on until that was done and so I lost time...A twelve week project ended up being about a nine month project." (And time is money in property).*

Darren – *"We crashed a car. It was all brand new stuff. We got an American out to help tune it and we'd done eight passes in this thing, it was brand new, and wrote it off. ... We got told we'd never come back. Two weeks later we'd come runner up in Queensland."*

Everybody fails but some use that failure as feedback to learn from and to drive them forwards, to springboard them to greater success. They get over their fears and go on to monumental success.

Bruce Sutphen, project manager for filmmaker James Cameron's Deepsea Challenger dive into the Mariana Trench, the deepest part of the world's oceans, said, *"They were not afraid to make mistakes, they didn't take things for granted."* The team used practice dives to learn, they analyzed the failures and used the experience to get it right.

Different people have different approaches. Those who have been through a major life-changing event such as bankruptcy, heart attack or stroke, will often have a more aggressive approach to setting and achieving goals.

Sharon Jurd is an accomplished Australian businesswoman. When Sharon ran a successful real estate business, she suffered a debilitating illness taking her away from her business for over a year. Sharon recovered and came back even stronger. She now runs a number of businesses and in 2014, the Franchise Council of Australia recognized her as Franchise Woman of the Year.

I know what it is like to be fear-driven, the fear of failing, fear of losing respect or even losing a job. Other indicators that you might experience fear of failure include:

- Doubting your capability in spite of evidence that you are capable; evidence such as past performance.

- Worrying about what other people think of you or about disappointing them.

- Lacking the confidence to pursue different goals and activities.

- Working exceedingly long hours and double and triple checking everything.

What worked for me was marshalling the fear and using it to drive my performance. Fear is an effective motivator, to a point. Fear is what I call "push in the back" motivation, where you are driven away from something (failure) rather than to something (a goal). Goal progression should be a "drawing forward" experience, pulling you to the desired outcome. Fear motivation has many downsides, including the effects on your health, reducing willingness to take risks or to be creative, and an inclination to do only what needs to be done to get it over with.

PLY: *Darren – "Doubt, as in financial doubts? Absolutely. Doubts that we could do what we wanted to do? Never."*

I was shy and on entering high school, I decided to do something about it. I attended the first session of a Toastmasters course. Toastmasters International is an organization for communication and leadership development. The toastmaster asked me to speak for two minutes about the army cadet program run in the school. I was not a cadet, so I had to think quickly about anything I knew. The instructor said I did very well and the class applauded. In spite of the success, the incident terrified me so much that I never returned. I let fear take a wonderful opportunity away from me. I was afraid of failure. Many years later, I did several Dale Carnegie courses and loved them.

PLY: *Tony says, "I used to have a fear of failure but I actually enjoy it because I actually know there is no such thing as failure. It is how you define it. I realize that, essentially, we are just on a journey of character development."*

Jacqui *says, "Essentially, I do not believe anything actually is a failure. At any given time, most people will use as much info as they can to make a decision... Later on, new information may come to them or their awareness which may influence them and they may make another decision but the last one was not wrong or a failure."*

Many, maybe most, people, experience fear when they are outside their comfort zone. Many let it take opportunities away. Many others face the fear and achieve, sometimes because of it and sometimes in spite of it. An example from my home state of Queensland, Australia, is champion football player Darren Lockyer. "*Every time I go to a game I always have that fear of losing or a sense of failure,*" he said in an AAP interview before retiring in 2011. This did not prevent Darren from setting many records as a club, state and national player.

Exercises for Dealing with Fear

The secret to using fear positively in "drawing forward" goal progression is to face it. This brings it to the conscious and reduces its subconscious effect. In addressing your fears, you will feel them, for we are good at visualizing the negative. You feel the physiological changes in your body (muscle tension, increased heart rate, sweating and nervousness) because your brain cannot tell the difference between reality and the vividly imagined. Perhaps your fear is failing to complete a task on time at work or having to make calls to customers, or perhaps you are scared of the changes wealth or success might bring. Initial fear, such as when you have a scare, is a reaction to the source of fear. Afterwards, it is a feeling and you can change feelings.

PLY: *How Jacqui handles fear – "I talk to my closest confidantes about the fear that is associated with whatever it is. When we're talking, we look at 'what is the worst that can happen' then use Socratic questioning – 'then what would happen?', and 'then what would happen?', until you drill down to the point that nothing will actually happen. I also then visualise how I want it to pan out."*

Find a quiet and relaxing space where you will not be disturbed. Being in a quiet, safe place will allow you to deal with the fears. Sit with a pen and paper. Stop if you feel too much distress.

1. Think of the fear and conjure up a situation that raises the fear. Think only about the fear and not any solutions. Don't evaluate the fear by saying it is silly or irrational.

2. Write down the issues, the causes and what you feel.

3. Think about the worst that can happen because of the fear. Let yourself feel where the tension is in your body (neck, shoulders, stomach, etc.).

4. Write down these consequences.

5. Write down as many ideas as you can to prevent or deal with the situation, should it occur. Don't assess them or limit them, just write them down.

6. Select the top five actions and write down the pros and cons of each.

7. Select the two best ones and think about how you can put them in place; what steps are required. Think about the best course of events you can achieve and use this to generate the expectation in your mind, the goal. Having two strategies gives you choice.

8. As a measure, check back with your body – How are you feeling now? Have the symptoms reduced?

9. Act! Ultimately, thinking may not cure fear but action does (going through this exercise may dispel some of the fear). Don't focus on the fear; focus on the first step, then the second step and so on.

10. Once you have read Chapter 6 on visualization, revisit this exercise and enhance your action plan. Use your goal setting imagination techniques to make them happen, to look for shortcuts and to measure against your expectation.

This exercise works because:

1. You think about the actual fear, rather than suppressing it. This brings it into the light and often shows it to be less powerful than expected.

2. You sit there with the feeling, understanding where the feeling is in your body and "talking" to it (this might be a little unnerving at first). Understand that the feeling will not overwhelm you.[v]

3. You formulate your plan of attack and take action.

4. This brings you certainty, and certainty brings courage. You know how to deal with the issue if it arises.

5. Mostly, the worst thing that can happen rarely does.

Another effective technique for dealing with worry and fear is to delay your response to it. When appropriate, say to yourself, "I'll worry about that at 2pm tomorrow" or "I'll worry about that in 10 minutes." This is your delay script. At that nominated time, go back and think about your worries but until then, if they arise, use the delay script. This takes out the initial reaction and enables you to think more clearly. It will also get you through until you can address them.

Marc Miles, a Gold Coast trainer and entrepreneur, dealt with his reluctance to speak to strangers. Marc spoke to big groups for a living, but one-on-one with a complete stranger was daunting. So, Marc kept a daily tally of every stranger he talks to or gets to smile at him, "count the strangers." Marc is now finding that people will approach him and talk to him. Marc faced his fear by making it into a game.

Dealing with Stress

For many, the act of setting a goal and putting a timeframe on it can cause feelings of tension and stress. As deadlines approach and progress has not kept pace, these feelings can arise. This stress can come from a fear of failure, fear of letting others down, or even fear of success when you don't believe you can play at that level (see Imposter Syndrome in Chapter 2).

The options, when it comes to fear, are to run away from it or use it as a driver. Procrastination is the run-away option, where you will do other things to distract yourself from the stress, which further impedes progress and increases the risk of failure.

Let's turn this around. The tension is a driver; it is a motivator for you to act. You achieve motivation in two ways. The first is to move away from discomfort, push-in-the-back motivation, or move towards something pleasant or pull-forward motivation. Both work and you can use both. Having a clear and compelling goal is pull-forward motivation and stress and tension are push-in-the-back motivators.

> **"Life can be pulled by goals just as surely as it can be pushed by drives."**
> Viktor E. Frankl – Austrian Neurologist,
> Psychiatrist and Holocaust Survivor, 1905-1997

One role of your subconscious is to protect you. The tension is your subconscious keeping you congruent and in harmony with your thoughts and decisions. You said you were going to do something by a certain date and you are not doing it so your subconscious gives you the warning signals to motivate you to act (it is called cognitive dissonance). In the same way you get a feeling you should avoid a dark alley, you are getting signals to protect you from feelings of failure, keeping you congruent with your decisions.

The tension will also come from warnings from your subconscious that you might fail, experience ridicule or lose your life savings. These come from previous experience, from feelings of long past events you no longer remember. Don't simply accept these warnings because the circumstances that created them may not be relevant. Analyze these warnings, do the "worst thing that can happen" exercise on them to extract the lessons and course of action and use the positive drive from them to set your goals. Accept these warnings as tools you can use to understand what's happening and control it. In *Chapter 4 – Using Your Subconscious*, we'll discuss feelings and emotions as a feedback and monitoring system.

To achieve, use the tension to motivate you, not to distraction and procrastination but to action. Taking action will make you feel good, increase confidence and motivate you to more action to get that good feeling again. Taking action turns push-in-the-back into pull-forward. Embrace it, look for it and love it, make that tension your friend. You can even make your timeframes tighter to generate tension and ride it to achievement.

A balance is required, though. Too much tension and stress will shut you down and reduce your creativity and productivity. If there is too much for the above techniques to manage, you will need to change something else. Putting yourself under pressure can impede learning. The reason work places conduct fire drills in buildings where people work is so that they learn the routine to exit the building safely when there is no pressure on them. This repetition enables them to repeat the actions when there is a fire emergency.

The success of goal setting shows that we are more inclined to get what we want, than not get what we don't want. In most cases we are doing both, moving away from pain (e.g., discomfort from not having or achieving) as we move towards pleasure (the pleasure of having or achieving).

PLY: *Graham's drive was to move away from the pain of his childhood circumstances to a successful environment that he created himself.*

Even with physical pain, we move away from the pain to the pleasure of pain relief. We may choose to go through some pain to get to the pleasure. Procrastination is a great example, where you put off doing a stressful task by doing something you like, or like better than the task, possibly to your later detriment (and more pain).

Fear can initiate change but it won't be sustainable and you will go back to the old ways. Dr. Edward D. Miller, Dean and CEO of Johns Hopkins Medicine, at the 2005 Global Medical Forum presented the findings on 600,000 people with severe heart disease who were told that if they didn't change their habits they would die. When revisited in 12 months, only 10% had changed.[vi] All bad news and a bad solution.

Dean Ornish, Clinical Professor of Medicine from the University of California and founder of the Preventive Medicine Research Institute, has been advocating the effects of diet and lifestyle change on heart disease for 25 years. Many medical insurance companies now offer his program to those diagnosed with heart disease. Dr. Ornish took a different view from Dr. Miller's, explaining to patients the benefits they would receive from following his program, rather than the consequences of not following it.[vii]

Your brain has a reward system that releases a neurochemical called dopamine, which generates positive feelings. The system controls your responses to rewards, such as achievement, foods, music, sex and laughter. It makes you feel good. Dopamine also triggers the memory cells and is essential to learning and long-term memory. When dopamine is produced it tells your memory centers to pay attention to the experience so that what you did can be repeated in the future (you want more of what you like).

The lesson from this is to frame your goal in terms of what you will gain, not what you will lose. We will cover the framing of goals in Chapter 9. Fear and stress as motivators do work but it is healthier, more sustainable and achieves improved results if you can turn the negative into a positive. Practice the techniques in this book without pressure, to allow you to repeat them confidently when you need to perform, when you need the drive or to make a deadline.

However, don't sell yourself short. People have done amazing things under the pressure of incredible deadlines and driven by outrageous goals. It is in you to do that too.

Carolyn Cranwell, author of *"Navigating Alzheimer's Survival Secrets of a Long Term Carer,"* spent many years looking after her husband as early onset dementia took him away from her. Every day there were new challenges brought up by her husband's illness for which Carolyn had to develop solutions. While caring for her husband and raising her children, Carolyn realized she had to be the breadwinner, so she had to continue working as her husband could not stay in the workforce. Whenever a challenge arose, she would ask herself, "Is it possible that this can be done? If the answer is **YES**, I will do it. If the odds are 100 to 1, I choose to be that **one**." This is a great technique to use for yourself.

Dealing with Procrastination

I procrastinated when writing this section. I had written the rest of this chapter and six others before I came back to this section. You will recognize from personal experience, the main attributes of procrastination. Various researchers have confirmed these attributes.[viii]

1. We have a commitment to perform the action (we can't say "forget about it") as the outcome has value.

2. We only want to do what we like to do, we will put off less pleasant activities (which psychologists call aversive) in favor of actions we would prefer (or prefer to do instead of the action in question).

3. We want big results and we want them now. We will take actions providing a more immediate outcome (reward) over those taking longer.

4. We voluntarily delay the action (otherwise it is not procrastination but another obstacle).

5. We will delay actions where we are not confident in our ability to deliver the outcome.

6. We are sidetracked by other issues in our lives, causing loss of focus.

7. We will work harder when closer to a deadline if there is a negative impact on us if we miss it.

For me, it was about analyzing why I procrastinate, when I do it and why I do it. As I hadn't done that work, I put off writing this section because I was not confident that I could deliver the outcome. Once I was prepared, I started and once I started, the words came.

Piers Steel from the University of Calgary says impulsiveness drives procrastination. Impulsiveness, in the form of both intense cravings or lack of perseverance, is critical to understanding why we procrastinate[ix]. Focusing on the future helps reduce impulsiveness. Focusing on the future is a key activity in achieving a goal. In *Chapter 6* you will learn how to thinkualize a future goal and how to make the future clear in your head, so clear that you can feel it. Research by Dr. Tim Pychyl from Carleton University in Canada has confirmed that focusing on your future intentions reduces the impact of impulsive behavior that would take you away from the desired goal. This all makes sense, doesn't it?

Researchers think of procrastination as an intention-action gap. They key point here is intention. If you intend to do it but you delay it unnecessarily, you are procrastinating. What if you don't intend to do it? If you have decided not to do it and you don't, that's not procrastination, obviously. However, if you know you should do it but are putting it off, you're procrastinating.

One solution to procrastination is simple – get started. The action of starting, regardless of our emotional state at the time, gives us the drive to do the task or at least make some progress. The task then does not seem as bad and, in fact, often becomes enjoyable as we are making progress towards achieving. If we have not completed the task, once we have made progress, it is easier to start the next time. A good way to start next time is to review what you have already done. That progress will give you confidence.

PLY: *Tiffany – "You don't want to set your deadlines too far in the future because you'll end up procrastinating. This is called Parkinson's Law." (Work expands to fill the time available for its completion).*

If the task is daunting and is causing procrastination, spend the time breaking it into smaller, achievable tasks. Setting a goal too far out in time with no sub-goals encourages procrastination as you seem to have all of the time in the world.

The point is that you are starting! Starting gives you the instant gratification you may need and a boost to your self-confidence coming from making progress.

In each of these cases, starting the task is a valid solution. Once we start, we will be more likely to like the task. Once started and progress is made, our confidence increases and we get positive feedback from making progress (a level of gratification). Starting a task can change your perception of the task from dislike to like.

PLY: *Coral, on steps in a property deal – "Sometimes I think, 'Ah, this is going to be really hard,' but then I just take small snapshots of what I've got to do. OK, I've got to go to the council, talk to them and if it's OK, I'll go back and I'll do the figures on it and then I'll make the offer and then… do step one, step two."*

Joanne, *on sub-goals – "Without the end goal you wouldn't bother with the micro-goals but I find the micro-goals incredibly rewarding."*

Tiffany – *"This was when I began to establish milestones and smaller goals along the way. One goal was to transfer from my local community college to a major university. Another goal was to see a therapist and make the most out of my experience."*

Sometimes procrastination can be a good thing. Procrastination can be your subconscious sending signals to you. It is worth considering those to see if there are some problems ahead you haven't consciously acknowledged.

A little procrastination may slow activities down, enabling you to develop better ideas. Professor Jihae Shin, at the University of Wisconsin, and Professor Adam Grant, at the Wharton School of the University of Pennsylvania, did some research to show that, of subjects given a task, those delaying a little, rather than jumping straight in, produced results that were 28% more creative. Leaving the task to the last minute however, produced poor results. You might say that wasn't procrastination but delay. Procrastination on this chapter helped me find this research.

In a New York Times article, Adam Grant said Steve Jobs and Bill Clinton were chronic procrastinators. Frank Lloyd Wright, architect, procrastinated for a year on what became Falling Water, his masterpiece. Aaron Sorkin, the screenwriter, doesn't call it procrastination; he calls it "thinking". These people did achieve but there were consequences to their procrastination.

However, a word of caution – progress can also backfire on you. Have you ever started a task, made progress and, at a point where it got a little harder, decided to take a break and congratulate yourself on the progress? In so doing, you have reduced the drive that got you there in the first place. The way to address this is to frame your progress as a step to the goal, remind yourself of the goal and your desire to achieve it, and keep going. Another way to get started is to commit a certain time to the task, say 10 minutes. Chances are, after 10 minutes, you will still be going.

In *Chapter 7 – Path Setting*, we will teach you Implementation Affirmations which help you identify the situations in which you procrastinate and how to make an action affirmation so your subconscious automatically acts to get you over the issue.

Action Statements

1. Do the exercises in facing fear and delaying fear on pages 51 to 53 for dealing with a fear preventing you from achieving your goals.

2. Follow these steps to manage the stress in setting a goal:

    a) Break the goal into steps – Bite off what you can chew. Achieving the smaller steps gives you confidence.

    b) Focus on the smaller steps – This distracts you from the huge effort (but not the goal) and keeps you making progress. Focus on the current step you are working on (see Chapter 8 on timeframes) and not the entire scary workload required to complete the goal.

c) Tick off each step when complete and acknowledge that fact to your-self, reinforcing the feelings of achievement. With the bigger mile-stones, plan some reward for yourself for achieving it (see Celebrate in Chapter 9).

d) Keep the final goal in mind in all its glory to remind you why you are doing this – use the thinkualization methods of Chapter 8 to stay moti-vated.

e) Review your timeframes and adjust any that are impractical – we dis-cuss elastic goals in *Chapter 9 – Constructing Your Goals*.

3. Don't simply accept the warnings from your subconscious. Analyze these warnings, do the "worst thing that can happen" exercise on them.

4. Use the tension you feel to motivate you to action. Turn push-in-the-back motivation into pull-forward motivation.

5. When procrastinating, identify the cause from the list on page 57 to help you address it. There may be other things happening that are affecting your focus.

6. Focus on the future to reduce impulsiveness, which is a key factor in pro-crastination.

7. The solution to procrastination is simple – Get started!

a) A good way to start next time is to review what you have done.

b) Break the goal into smaller tasks. Starting the task is a valid solution.

c) Commit a certain time to the task, say 10 minutes.

CHAPTER
4

Using Your
Subconscious

CHAPTER 4

Using Your Subconscious

*"Trust your instinct to the end,
though you can render no reason."*
Ralph Waldo Emerson – American Essayist, Lecturer and Poet

*"Your feelings are the summary of all of your thoughts at any
point in time. You can change your thoughts."*
Chris Christoff

There are many books and videos available for self-improvement that build on one fundamental idea – you are what you think. Many expound the benefits of positive self-talk for driving the required actions for achievement, for jumping the hurdles and dodging the obstacles life will inevitably put in your path. Positive self-talk has driven many great achievers to success, from scientists to business people to athletes. Positive self-talk is the mechanism you use to program your subconscious to work towards (not against) the goals of your conscious mind.

In this chapter, we explore how your subconscious works, how it drives decision-making and how to program the target outcomes you consciously want. For the sake of this discussion we will use the phrases "the unconscious" and "the subconscious" interchangeably.

The thinking on the workings of the mind and the concept of the subconscious has changed from the theories of Freud and Jung. Nobel Prize laureate, Daniel Kahneman, has theorized through his research a different view of how the brain forms thoughts. In his book, *"Thinking, Fast and Slow"* Kahneman discusses two systems. System 1 is Subconscious – fast, automatic, frequent and emotional. System 2 is Conscious – slow, effortful, infrequent, logical and calculating. The important point is that the subconscious works faster than the conscious, works automatically and is emotional. System 2 can program System 1 to notice patterns (System 1 detects change and irregularity exceptionally well), and train it for skilled intuition.

Dr. Ap Dijksterhuis[x] conducted experiments to measure the effectiveness of the unconscious brain in its decision-making abilities. Participants in three groups had to choose between different alternatives in different ways. The researchers asked the first group to produce an immediate decision, the second group to take time for conscious thought, and gave the third group the problem but then distracted them by another task. The results showed that the unconscious decisions were the best.

Further research on this by Alex Pouget, an associate professor of brain and cognitive sciences at the University of Rochester, has shown that people make the best decisions only when their unconscious brain makes the choice. Pouget says most of the decisions you make aren't based on conscious reasoning, "*You don't consciously decide to stop at a red light or steer around an obstacle in the road.*" Many of us have experienced driving home from work and arriving and not remembering anything about the trip, as we were thinking about something else. Our subconscious drove us home.

I have a personal example of this, what I call the mind's autopilot. When I was about 15 years old, I stayed with my grandmother for the Christmas break and my uncle was there. He could be strict and intolerant. There were two bottles of my uncle's soda (softdrink) on top of the fridge. I shut the fridge door a bit too forcefully and they both toppled forward off the fridge. They were glass bottles, so when they hit the floor they would smash into a million pieces and there would be mess everywhere.

They didn't. They didn't hit the floor. Before I knew what had happened I stood there with each hand grasping the neck of a bottle. I had caught them. Had I thought about what I should do, they would have hit the floor. I was motivated to one goal – the bottles must not hit the floor. I had a clear goal, no idea of the journey, only the outcome and the result was driven by my subconscious.

PLY: *Joanne* *"You've also got to relax. I like meditation as a tool for going inside and helping to get in touch with the line of certain things ... And also for insights, you know, how it works with brushing your teeth or pulling weeds out... you get this brilliant idea and you're relaxed and you're not thinking about it."*

Tiffany – *"If we allow ourselves to surrender and listen to our intuition, we are given the wisdom we need. We need to be able to sit quietly without any distractions and just be. This is how I received my guidance."*

Axel Cleeremans[xi], a Professor of Cognitive Science Université Libre de Bruxelles, proposed in his "radical plasticity" thesis the idea that the conscious brain is a product of unconscious brain's continuous attempts at predicting the consequences of its actions. Thinking and reasoning are the unconscious mind's ability to process countless possibilities and predict the consequences of taking a certain course of action, while the conscious mind is only able to process the outcomes of a couple of courses of action to make decisions.

This work shows how adept the subconscious is at driving decisions. In motivating yourself to reach your goals, a key tool for your success is the programming of your unconscious to help you get the work done. BUT, that does not mean you don't think about the goal and what you are doing or make conscious decisions. I prefer to have my "System 2" have a look over what my "System 1" decides. Also, Kahneman's testing shows "System 1" tends to make overconfident predictions because it makes the judgement from the best story it can construct from the evidence at hand and it believes it. In that case, give your System 1 more information by thinking and remembering. In the chapter on visualization, we will explore how to construct thinkualizations to achieve this programming.

Our subconscious needs to finish what we start, which works well for us when we set goals. Identified by Russian psychologist Bluma Zeigarnik in 1927, the Zeigarnik Effect is the tendency to keep thinking about a goal that was not completed. The automatic system in our subconscious keeps reminding us to get back on track and finish the goal.

What else does your subconscious do for you? In terms of the role of the subconscious, there are a number of beliefs about how it works. See how these relate to your own experience.

Activities of the Subconscious

Stores and Categorizes Memory – Your beliefs and values come from the influences throughout your life, both encouraging and traumatic. Your subconscious records the memories and associated feelings and they influence your behavior and actions long after you cannot consciously recall the original memory. Have you experienced liking or disliking something, or somebody, but not remembering a clear reason for the feeling?

The subconscious filters your experiences through your beliefs and values, and creates your perception of the world. It is only a perception and you can change it. You can change your perceptions about your ability to set goals and achieve.

Senses and Bodily Function – The subconscious takes in the information from your senses, interprets meaning and triggers awareness when required (e.g., is the sensation on your arm a bug crawling on you?). The subconscious response to both internal and external stimuli can affect various physical functions such as heart rate, breathing, muscle tension and stomach reactions. The most notable examples are stress, fear and excitement and we all know the physiological effects of these.

Your conscious thought can influence your subconscious, which in turn influences bodily function, such as reducing stress and heart rate through mental concentration. The placebo effect, where the doctor prescribes a non-active (fake) medicine or procedure for psychological benefit to the patient, is well known. Researchers have found such treatments can stimulate real physiological responses, from changes in heart rate and blood pressure, to chemical activity in the brain in cases involving pain, depression, anxiety, fatigue and even some symptoms of Parkinson's.[xii]

Using the senses (sight, hearing, taste, touch, smell, temperature and proprioception (knowing where your body is in space)) can be powerful tools in strengthening your goal setting. We will cover this in *Chapter 6 – Visualizing Your Goals – The Art of Thinkualization.*

Self-Preservation – The subconscious activates the fight or flight mechanism when the body is threatened, that feeling you get when you are about to go into a dark alley or your reaction to jump out of the path of an oncoming bus. This can go overboard, as seen in people with panic disorder where their subconscious threat detection can lead to misinterpretations and false alarms but for most of us, this is an effective protection mechanism.

Communicates through Emotions, Feelings, Intuition – The subconscious uses emotions and feelings as signals to tell you what is going on. Feelings of fear, embarrassment, happiness, envy, excitement and so on all give you information on what is happening. The feelings are signals of your reactions and a response to what you are thinking. The self-protection mechanism, along with using the emotions and feelings as indicators of what is happening in your head, provides a feedback system for keeping you on track in your goal advancement.

Feelings and emotions are your indicators of thoughts, telling you whether the thoughts are positive or negative. There are no "bad" feelings, they are telling what you are thinking and indicate whether action is required. With you arguably having over 60,000[5] thoughts per day, it's not possible for you to monitor every thought to ensure you are working on your required outcomes. Feelings are the summaries of these thoughts at any one point in time and allow you to assess the overall theme of your thoughts.

PLY: *Jacqui on dealing with the negative – "I'll go through a process of thinking it through, checking myself. Checking myself emotionally, like 'is there an emotional reaction to this?' Often there is….sitting, listening, processing, checking myself. Is that in me? Where is that in me? If I can't find it, letting it go."*

---

5. There are no reliable sources for this number but it is popular. Daniel Kahneman says 600,000 per month.

In my work in IT, we built mission-critical data systems, important to the correct operations of the company. These systems had to be reliable and they consisted of many components with networks, servers, databases and applications, each with a multitude of subcomponents.

We implemented monitoring systems to track the operation of every component but we people cannot deal with the millions of pieces of information generated about the health of the systems. We needed a summary; we needed the monitoring to gives us a feeling about the health of the systems, so we used a traffic light indicator – green is good and we are on track, yellow is a warning and we can decide if action is needed and red is bad and we take action to fix the problem. In the same way, you can use your feelings to monitor yourself and determine if you are in the green, yellow or red.

Cleeremans[xi] makes the comment at the end of his paper that emotion is crucial to learning, for there is no sense in which anyone would learn about anything if the learning failed to *do something* to them.

Intuition

Intuition, to understand something without conscious reasoning, is also a feeling. While instinct relates more to an innate behavior, because people relate to the phrase "a gut instinct," we will use the words instinct and intuition interchangeably. I don't believe these instincts or intuitions are the universe calling you – I believe the magic comes from within you. Instincts are your brain processing all of the cues in your surroundings and in your subconscious and providing you with the feelings as indicators.

If you are like me, where everything has to be analyzed and the numbers stack up, trusting your intuition is something you will have to learn. I am sure you would have had this experience: You took a path contrary to your initial intuition, plans did not go as projected and you thought, "I knew I should have gone with my instincts." If you have done this, you're on the right track. You can refine this skill. The effectiveness of gut instinct to assist clinical decision-making has even been researched in veterinary science and cancer diagnosis.

PLY: *Carol Wheatley's experience – "We had a gut feeling [for a deal] and we didn't go with that gut feeling. We knew we shouldn't have gone for it and it turned out to be a bad decision. If it doesn't go with your gut feeling, then you shouldn't go with it".*

Dr X – *(on reasons for failure) – "There's a lack of congruence between what their head's telling them to do and what their body-mind is telling them to do. We do have to be in alignment....There's a sad gap between how we're brought up now, not trusting that deep inner-knowing...We're very good at tuning out of our intuition."*

Joanne – *"...intuition plays a big part ... you can't just go blindly by gut instinct, because you've got to do research and work on facts, but that instinct can take you a long way and can also help you make better decisions when faced with two options."*

Kawena *relates the solar plexus feeling of gut instinct to the soul, the soul saying, "We don't want to go there."*

Autopilot

Consider the power of this statement – *"Routines, by allowing actors (people) to make many decisions at a subconscious level, conserve cognitive power (thinking) for non-routine activities."* This is the finding in a paper by Prof Trisha Greenhalgh on work routines in healthcare organizations.[xiii]

Imagining what you want, and continually refining your thinkualization, allows you to program your autopilot to get to where you want to go. You make errors or make changes and refinements as you clarify the vision and you adjust accordingly. However, no autopilot does anything without one important thing – motion! You need action; you need to do something. Thinkualize and do, refine, thinkualize, do.

You won't need to do everything perfectly the first time. Keep trying, keep moving forward, making errors and correcting them. How do you think you catch a ball? Your nervous system continually makes corrections to the positions of your muscles, correcting errors until your hand is in the correct place.

Those who can catch well can do so because they have practiced, training the automatic mechanism to do the right thing. The training is achieved through trying, failing and trying again.

Carolien Hermans, a PhD student at the Theatre Studies Department of Utrecht University, said in a paper, "The reaction time of dancers is much faster when driven by the lower process of control, which is rapid, subconscious and automatic. The professional body can gain speed and accuracy by training automatic responses."

The seminal work on training the subconscious is Psycho-Cybernetics by Dr. Maxwell Maltz, published in 1960 with over 30 million copies sold (that's over 40,000 copies per month for 56+ years). Dr. Maltz was the first plastic surgeon to try to understand why people wanted surgery and why it sometimes didn't change their beliefs about themselves. Dr. Maltz spent the latter part of his career talking people out of surgery and working on their mindset. His book discusses the brain's built-in goal striving mechanism, which he labels the Automatic Success Mechanism. By training the brain it can be the autopilot to deliver the required outcome, whether this is a golfer visualizing the flight of the ball, and its landing at the green, before making the swing, or a businessman preparing for a sales meeting; it's all about the programming.

You act and perform in accordance with what you believe about yourself and your environment. Your nervous system reacts to what you think to be true, whether it is or not. Imagine stepping into the house at night in the dark and turning on the light to see a large snake on the floor. Whether the snake is alive or made of rubber, your subconscious will react the same way. You will get a rush of adrenaline and jump away from it.

The automatic goal-seeking machine must have a target; whether that is the ball in the air you are catching or the goal of owning your own house. By focusing on the target and clearly experiencing the target in your mind, you can take the conscious actions and allow the automatic success mechanism to take care of the rest.

Action Statements

Action:

1. Develop your intuition – take a scientific approach:

    a) Write down what you feel about the issue now and what your "gut" tells you before the analysis

    b) Go and do what you usually do

    c) When the issue has been resolved, revisit your notes and see how close you were

    d) Keep doing this until the gap reduces and you can trust your gut feelings

    e) During the day, pay more attention to what is happening and how you feel. This will provide more information for both your conscious and subconscious to use to guide your decision-making

2. Program your unconscious to help you get the work done and to change your perceptions about your ability to set goals and achieve:

    a) Train by thinkualizing the actions and outcomes.

    b) Train by trying, failing and trying again.

    c) Keep trying, keep moving forward, making errors and correcting them.

3. Feelings are the summaries of your thoughts at any one point in time. Use your feelings to monitor yourself and determine if you are in the green, yellow or red.

CHAPTER
5

What Do You Want?

CHAPTER 5

What Do You Want?

"What you want to do and what you can do, is limited only by what you can dream."
Mike Melville – US Aviator, Astronaut, 1940-

"Exploring what you want can be daunting, for fear of not achieving it, but to achieve it you must explore."
Chris Christoff

In this chapter, we'll spend a little time exploring some of the types of goals you might like to set. Goals can be set in many areas of your life and they can be small or large, near-term or in the distant future. You can set a goal in any area of your life and pursue any passion.

You may not have a passion but you may be good at something and this talent may lead you to a passion. Your passion may uncover hidden talents. Think about the passions and talents you had as a child and as a teenager and explore them for ideas for goals that inspire you.

PLY*: Tony Gattari wanted to be the CEO of a publically listed company. He achieved the goal and hated it. He realised he had no passion for the business, as he was not using his strengths and talents and was not focused on his gifts.*

Coral's *first passion was food. Circumstances changed and her passion changed to real estate. "Really it's still what we eat, sleep, drink, talk about with our family and it's just something we've grown to be confident in."*

Darren – *"Passion is everything. People will say it's money, well it's not money because with passion you'll find money or a backer or sell your* *house and go and do it. ... If you are passionate, passionate people will follow you. None of our guys got paid, no-one. We won 3 championships and nobody got paid."*

Joanne – *"I grew up with an absolute passion for horses and ponies and I wanted my own pony from the moment I knew what one was."*

Kawena *says when she mentors people, "I help them get their confidence back, work on their talents. People don't know what they are good at, what the talents are they were born with."*

Personal Development

Personal development goals are often a good place to start or to run in parallel with other goals. Personal development can help provide the skills and attributes that enable and empower you to set and achieve other goals in your life. Explore the attributes you have and those you want or need and use this list to set your PD goals. Review the links to sets of traits in the *Resources* section and the table of assets and liabilities in the *Know Your Starting Point* resource on the website.

You might consider the skills and attributes needed to achieve current or future goals such as communication skills to engage others, project management skills for a project, or working on your confidence. Self-development should be a continual, unending process for you, regardless of the other goals you set in life.

PLY: *Tiffany has used the things she learned from Tony Robbins, "I visualized what I wanted to create in my life. I focused on my core values and how I wanted to live my life. I looked at every aspect of my life – relationships, health and nutrition, career and personal development – and began to envision the kind of lifestyle I wanted to experience. I can honestly [say] that I'm living that lifestyle today."*

Possessions and Toys

This category could be the most fun as you think about what you want in life. If you don't have goals in this area, this might be a fun place to start. One way to find out what you want is to find out what's out there. For toys like cars and boats (admit it, they are toys) go to a dealer, several dealers, and check them out. Review their specifications on the web and learn about their capabilities and options. Attend car shows or boat shows in your area if you have them. Get photos of yourself in the car or boat to use to motivate your actions. If you're not into toys, for the more personal items like jewelry and clothing, go to retailers and try them on, see how they look and take photos of yourself wearing them.

Check out magazines on the things you like – car, 4WD, camping, boating, yachting, planes or audiovisual systems magazines. There are magazines for nearly everything. For the best money can buy, check out the Robb Report, http://robbreport.com/ which covers cars, boats, planes, helicopters, fashion, jewelry and much more.

Health and Fitness

Health and fitness are among the most common categories for goal setting. The opportunities are many, from losing weight to simple healthy eating, from lowering body fat to increasing muscle strength. Fitness goals may include training for a sport, or training for an event such as running a marathon. Maybe your goal is to reduce your blood pressure, increase your flexibility or increase your reps at the gym. You might learn a new physical skill such as dancing or a martial art. Goal setting can pull you through an illness, or help to put your life together after an extended illness.

In this category, there is a lot of material on the internet and there are many health, fitness and beauty resources available.

Houses and Homes

In most of the world, home ownership is a primary goal of many people. Buying a house is one of the largest purchases most people will ever make. Home ownership in many parts of the world is increasingly more difficult due to economic factors and increasing house prices. This is the case in Australia at present. Home ownership in some European countries is low in comparison with other parts of the world. Many would like to live in a large, beautiful house but you have to start somewhere. The best way to get into the real estate market is, well, to get into the real estate market by buying what you can afford and working your way to where you would like to be. If home ownership is not practical for you, a suitable goal may be the rental of a desirable property.

Vacations and Experiences

Experiences and places to visit around the world are high on people's bucket lists. Planning for a vacation or holiday is a great goal setting experience. Saving the money, taking the time away from job and commitments, planning the destinations and itinerary are all steps in setting the goal for a fantastic reward. There are opportunities to explore your own country and to travel the world, experiencing the food, languages and cultures.

Experiences are also great goals. They can be part of a vacation or embarked on separately. Experiences make travel so much more memorable and there are experiences for every personality and pocket – museums and galleries in Europe, ancient ruins in Greece and Egypt, balloon ride over the geological oddities of Cappadocia or you can trek the Incan ruins of Machu Picchu in Peru. You can dive and see the sea life of the Great Barrier Reef, have clothes made in Hoi Ann in Vietnam, take a private trans-Siberian train ride or a cooking lesson with a celebrity chef. Race a Lamborghini around the Imola racetrack in Italy or register for a Virgin Galactic flight. There is so much to experience.

Family and Relationships

Relationships are an area of life in which you can set goals. If you are seeking a partner, you can set goals on the attributes you want in your partner, how you might meet them and how the relationship will develop. The attributes might include qualities you don't have but would like in another. You could look at previous failed relationships, work out why they failed and use that information.

If you're in a relationship, you can set goals to improve the relationship, including quality time, communication (talking and listening), honesty, trust, regular date nights and rewards, joint goals, goals with your children and relationships with others in the family. Events within families can be goals, such as marriages (yours or your child's), special Christmas or significant event celebrations and family holidays.

Career and Business

A career is a huge part of most peoples' lives and many merely fall into something without much planning. People mostly decide on their career directions while they're still at school but adults can also redirect their lives on a new course. Career goals can extend to starting a business, entering a profession, learning new skills, achieving qualifications or seeking promotions. You might have targets to reach or exceed or productivity increases you can attain. Career goals may also be advancement goals within your current business or profession.

You can set goals to develop your people management skills and style by deciding what type of manager you want to be, work out the attributes of that type, and set goals to develop those attributes. This is powerful as you choose your style and this will give you confidence in the workplace.

Young people often make career decisions while at school and should be taught how to set goals for their life achievement. For Gen Ys, I can recommend the book, *"Awesome Careers for Gen Ys"* by Sharon Davey. This book will also give employers insight into Gen Ys' workplace expectations and motivation.

Finance and Investments

Do you think about receiving checks (cheques) in the mail? If want checks in the mail, you will need a source of income – dividends from shares in the stock market, property rental income, an internet business, a long lost rich uncle or a winning lottery ticket that pays installments. To get "checks in the mail" you will require a passive income, unlike a job in which you trade hours for dollars.

Finance and investment goals can form the platform for many subsequent goals, providing the money for lifestyle, experiences and possessions. The range of investment vehicles is vast and can be put into various categories and types including buying shares or businesses, real estate, precious metals, collectables, cash, bonds, venture capital and loans you make to others, investment trusts, commodities, foreign exchange and even shipping containers. You can base investment goals on achieving a certain return on the money you invest. If you buy an asset you might make money by selling it or through the income it earns. Goal-based investing is an investment methodology that measures the result by how well the investment meets your personal and lifestyle goals.

There are many magazines and online resources for ideas for investments. These resources can teach you the best ways to navigate the possible pitfalls and risks. Obtain good professional advice and do your homework first so that you ask good questions and understand the answers.

Action Statements

1. Think about the passions and talents you had as a child and as a teenager and explore them for ideas for goals that inspire you.

2. Review the links to sets of traits in the *Resources* section and the table of assets and liabilities in the *Know Your Starting Point* resource on the website.

3. Review the types of goals in this chapter and decide what is out there for you.

CHAPTER
6

Visualizing Your Goals – The Art of Thinkualization

CHAPTER 6

Visualizing Your Goals – The Art of Thinkualization

> *"You must understand that seeing is believing but also know that believing is seeing."*
> Denis Waitley – Former Chairman of Psychology on the
> U. S. Olympic Committee's Sports Medicine Council, 1933-

> *"You have to see your way clear to see your way clear."*
> Chris Christoff

What is Thinkualization?

> *"Visualize this thing that you want, see it, feel it, believe in it. Make your mental blue print and begin to build."*
> Robert Collier – American Author, 1885-1950

Did your parents read you stories when you were a kid? Did you see the characters in your head, see the pirates on the roiling seas, hear the roar of the dinosaurs, feel the distress of the damsel, feel the power of the magic, reel at the actions of the villains or celebrate with the heroes? If so, you have visualized, you have thinkualized.

Visualization is the process of creating the image of a desired goal in your mind. Visualization, as the name implies, is visual, something you see. However, people create mental representations in different ways, just as they have different favored learning styles. Some people need to see something to learn it, others can be told how to do it and others need to do it themselves (feel it). Good learning systems will incorporate these different styles, both to appeal to an individual's primary learning mode but also to reinforce the learning through the other modes.

Some people have difficulty creating a visual picture in their minds, as they are not "visual" people. However, they can imagine the sounds and feelings (both emotion and touch) associated with an event or even remember through taste and smell. These together can powerfully describe a scene you may not have experienced in person but can experience in your mind. Use all of the senses and emotion for a powerful thinkualization – feelings and sight, hearing, taste, touch, smell, temperature and proprioception.

Which of these creates the more vivid picture in your mind?

1.   A gathering inside a house on a snowy Christmas day.

2.   The snow is falling outside, you are sitting on a soft rug in front of a fireplace, the warm fire crackles quietly, the taste of your favorite drink is on your lips, the smell of cooking food wafts through the house, as you chat with good friends you haven't seen in a while.

The second one creates a vivid experience, as it details triggers for all of your senses. It creates a story, reminding you of past experiences or it may create a new experience for you.

The term *thinkualization* refers to imaging using any or all of these perceptive modes, as visualization does not encompass them all. You can use all of these modes to create an image of a goal, to bring it to life and make it real. Your mind cannot distinguish between a real event and one vividly imagined. Your mind is abundantly powerful. There is an old cliché that says, "Radio: It's like TV but the pictures are better." How many have read a fantastic book then rushed off to see the movie only to be disappointed?

PLY: *Julius on goal setting – "[It is a] visual thing, of where I want to be, and see myself being".*

Dreaming and Dream Building

"To accomplish great things we must first dream, then visualize, then plan... believe... act!"
Alfred A. Montapert – American Philosopher, Author, 1906-1977

Dreaming … you need to dream … you must have a dream. You have heard it all before. You have read it in the self-help books and heard sports personalities and celebrities in interviews talk about it, but do you believe it? Even now you hear scientists and engineers talk about dreams.

The media reminds us all the time about those who took their dreams to reality. An obvious one is Walt Disney, a huge dreamer, and his entertainment empire. In the IT world, there is Steve Jobs and Apple, Bill Gates and Microsoft, Michael Dell and Dell Computer and Sergey Brin and Larry Page from Google. The motorcar industry gave us Henry Ford and Enzo Ferrari.

There was the massive dream of the US Kennedy government to put a man on the moon – Apollo XI. Architecture has brought us marvels such as Sheikh Mohammed bin Rashid Al Maktoum's Burj Khalifa building in Dubai, the tallest artificial structure in the world, and Antoni Gaudí's Sagrada Família in Barcelona. Retail brought us the giants of Wal-Mart, JC Penny, Tesco and Harrods. In every profession, in every walk of life there are dreamers who have set amazing goals and (failed and) succeeded. They were not only out to make money but also to follow their passions.

I come from an engineering and IT background with many years of project management. When planning an IT project, you set realistic goals based on realistic timeframes that come from analyzing the tasks required and resources available to achieve the goal, or from years of experience. These goals are set by knowing the path to your destination or by having the confidence that you can get there because you have done it many times before.

When it came to personal goals, I was the same. A goal was not a goal until I had planned the whole path and could see the journey and the destination. How could I set a goal if I didn't know how to achieve it or how long it would take to reach? I couldn't see the point of dreaming about stuff I could never have because I could not see the path to get it in a realistic way, so I could not set it as a goal. Stuck!

What I didn't understand then is that you can set "unrealistic" goals and you can achieve them, without first knowing how to do so. That is what dreaming is about. Dreaming gives you the "what" to which you add *why* you want it and the why comes from how it will affect your life, how you will feel and what it will do for others. We covered this in Chapter 2.

> **"Plan some, dream more."**
> Chris Christoff

Dream building is the process for building the desire for the goal, working out what you want and getting clarity about it. Use the thinkualization process to create a mental image to supplement your experiences in the physical world. If you want the dream home, go and look at houses and see what features they have that you like, read magazines and watch programs on beautiful homes. These kinesthetic experiences will reinforce the goal definition for you. For more information on dream-building resources, see Chapter 5.

The car I want to own is a Monte Carlo blue BMW X5 with champagne leather interior. To reinforce my dream for this car, I think about it, I thinkualize it. When I drive my current car (not a BMW) I am in the BMW, I can feel the steering wheel and smell the leather. I ignore the road noise because the BMW is quiet. I don't feel the road bumps, as the BMW has a superior ride with its adaptive suspension. The power of the visualization came to me when one day, after driving to the shop and ducking in for some groceries, I could not find where I parked my car. Why, my car is not blue. I was looking for a Monte Carlo blue car. This is how real dream building can be.

"I drive my dream car all of the time, my car doesn't know it yet."

The Lost Train Set

When I was very young, I lost a train set. I searched high and low looking for it. I looked in every cupboard, in the attic storage, under the house. I could not find it anywhere. I asked my mother if she had seen it and she told me I didn't have a train set. *"No, Mum, you are wrong, I did have one and I can't find it."* The reality was that I dreamt (actually and figuratively) about having this train set and the clarity was so intense that I "remembered" owning it, when in fact it was a visualisation. Maybe you think I was delusional. ☺

Association and Dissociation

Before getting into thinkualization we will cover these two important concepts.

When you are thinkualizing yourself in your goal, you are associating with the thinkualization. To internalize a thinkualization you must associate with it. This is a term used in NLP (Neuro Linguistic Programming) and means you are in the picture, not simply looking at yourself as if you are watching a movie of it. When you associate with the thinkualization, you are performing the actions and feeling the environment. You make the images and feelings close, bright and real. The association reinforces the goal.

If you view the goal as the reward and the things along the way as the actions and obstacles, you want a strong link between the work and the success. Dissociation is also a concept from NLP. As your mind cannot distinguish between a real event and one vividly imagined (remember the rubber snake), when you thinkualize something with great clarity your mind believes you already have it (see the Lost Train Set story in the box). In order for it to motivate you, your **subconscious must believe you are yet to achieve the goal**. This is important: you are yet to achieve it. There needs to be some tension set up between the goal and the reality and it is achieved through the dissociation technique. You need to dissociate from the goal enough to cause the tension, the motivation, to strive to achieve the goal, but not so much as to cease having the desire for the goal.

Dissociation is achieved through a mental process and is simply to see a picture in your mind of yourself experiencing the goal. You are not experiencing it; you are watching yourself experience it, as in a movie. You are not feeling the emotions of experiencing the goal. Do this after a session thinkualizing your goal, to keep that tension. Associate to reinforce, and then dissociate to create the drive.

Thinkualizing

Goal achievement is a two-stage process. The first stage is to set the primary goal and the second stage is striving to reach the goal. Goal setting is about – well, setting goals. You set the primary goal (the final destination) and then you set smaller goals that you need to achieve to take you along the path to reach the main objective. Small goals are simply stepping-stones to larger goals. First, you imagine the larger goal (the big picture) and apply the same technique to each of the steps required to get you there. Each of those smaller steps becomes a goal to achieve on the way. The path to achieve these smaller goals is your list of actions. We will cover the smaller goals in *Chapter 7 – Path Setting*.

The primary goal is the final desire and this provides both the direction for all of the actions along the path as well as the motivation and drive to perform the actions. It has to be clear and must trigger desires in you to be able to inspire you to keep on the path.

PLY*: Sharon Jurd visualises a primary goal two to five years out. She breaks this time into three-month intervals and visualises the smaller goals. From there, Sharon works out her actions and focuses on the 90-day period. Some of the time-distant goals may not be clear but as she* *progresses she clarifies them, always working in 90-day intervals. She is also always looking for opportunities to achieve a better outcome or to reach the end goal more quickly.*

Next, we will discuss how to create the picture of the goal to stimulate all of the senses you need to achieve the goal and to stay on track. These techniques are used to set any type of goal and we will cover some of the different types later in this chapter. Because the actions you need to take along the path to your goal are also goals, you use the same techniques to complete those actions. It is still possible to reach goals you have not clearly defined, by clearly setting a path, which we will cover in Chapter 7.

The House Example

Let's take something simple – $10,000,000. You have a desire for $10m bucks. How do you turn that into a dream? What would you do with $10m? Build a home?

The clarity comes from thinking about the outcome, experiencing it as if you have already achieved it, engaging all of your senses – knowing what it looks like and what it feels like. For this example, let's make some assumptions about the attributes of the home and you should substitute your own desires in this respect. Write your thinkualizations down so that you can define and refine them. When you read them you will refresh the vision in your mind.

PLY*: Joanne – "I think the more that I write things down ... it helps to visualize."*

Let's imagine you want to set a goal to acquire or build your dream home. The first step is to set the goal that you are going to have your dream home and then to define what this home will be like. What is in the home? Who lives in the house? Who visits? How do they feel being in the house? How do you feel walking through the house? Asking yourself these questions starts to formulate the dream.

Now, close your eyes and thinkualize how it feels to be in your dream house. Outside, you smell the scent of the trees in the garden. Hear the sound of the key in the lock as you enter through the front door. Feel the hair on your arms stand up because you are so excited and feel the gentle breeze blowing as you enter the house. Feel the weight of the doors and the notice the sound as they close and the sound of your footsteps as you walk on the timber floor. Notice how the light interacts with your chosen colors, hear the sound of friends having fun, notice the crackle and smell of the fireplace, feel the warmth as you stand in front of the fire, feel the carpet under your toes and see the morning light in the kitchen. You hear the sounds of the children playing in their bedroom; you feel the warm air flow through the home and experience the softness of the sofa in the living room. Go into the home theatre and watch the 60 inch TV – what is playing? Listen to the audio from your amazing sound system. You get the idea. Play with this idea for yourself and immerse yourself in your dream. Change the season to summer and walk through the thinkualization again. The more you do it, the clearer the picture will become.

At the end of the thinkualization, in your mind, step away from the house so you are observing it from outside and see yourself as if you are watching that movie. At this point, remember this is the goal, you have not achieved it yet but you are working towards it every day. This dissociation step is important. It is how you remind your subconscious that you must perform the actions to achieve the goal.

PLY: *It works differently for some people. Visualizing her psychology master's thesis as completed pushed Jacqui to start writing her thesis – "Doing that visualization ... pushed me to take action. Prior to that, I never did one thing. I didn't even look at one paper but the fact that my mind thought it was already done, pushed me to actually start doing it, to match the two together."*

This is a basic example and you could have more fun with it and get more clarity about this dream. Can you see that even with this basic example, you are creating a clarity of vision about what you want and the reasons why you want it? The reasons you want it will include how you feel when you have it, how others will relate to it, what you can do for others and how you can enjoy playing in it. The "why" helps build the "what."

Can you see that you have also turned a vague desire for $10m into a dream that ignites your passion? Of course, you can do others things with $10m and they should be the subject of more of your dreams. Thinking about having $10m, just the cash without a reason why, without thinking about what you would do with it, will not excite passion, at least for most people. In fact, you would probably find it difficult not to think about what you would do with $10m, so do what comes naturally and dream. For examples of other thinkualizations, see the *Thinkualizations* resource section on the website.

With this clarity, and once you have the reasons why, your continued thinkualization of this goal will influence your behavior and help you see and realize opportunities for achieving the goal. This example also shows you that you can thinkualize a goal without knowing the path to get there. Simple isn't it? Just let it happen …

PLY: *Donna – "My visual thing in my mind was running in the Melbourne Cricket Ground. It's a big thing to be running on the MCG and the visualization in my mind was having people cheer me, and my family being there, and friends, and I even thought maybe I'd have a tear or two and arms up in the air. The visualization is important, even the feeling, 'How will I feel?' "*

There are two other important aspects to achieving your goal – action, as we have already discussed, and a timeframe. We will discuss the timeframe in Chapter 8.

Uses of Thinkualization

Sport

Imagine yourself competing in an Olympic skiing event, as a slalom skier, an aerialist or on the bobsled team. The event is over in minutes and the world rushes by while you are performing, no time to think, only time to react. How do you deliver your best performance? Physical training establishes the skill and muscle memory and mental training instructs the subconscious to do what is required to achieve the outcome.

While athletes at the Winter Olympics in Sochi were waiting for their turn for the aerial event, they mentally rehearsed their performance. As they go through the event in their mind, the athlete's muscles will trigger as if they are actually performing the actions. Eyes closed, they will move and wave their arms around going through all of the required motions. *"Oh, yeah, it's ridiculous; we're all up there flapping our arms,"* veteran American aerialist Emily Cook is quoted in the New York Times as saying. *"It looks insane, but it works,"* she says referring to this mental rehearsal of a task in the absence of the actual physical movement.

During the 1980s, Dr. Denis Waitley served as Chairman of Psychology on the U. S. Olympic Committee's Sports Medicine Council, responsible for performance enhancement of all U. S. Olympic athletes. Waitley took visualization methods from the Apollo program into the Olympic program, introducing 'Visual Motor Rehearsal' into the Olympic program. Waitley's testing found that when an athlete competed in an event *only in their mind*, the same muscle-nerve stimulation occurred in the body as when they performed the event in real life. Waitley's research confirmed that the mind can't tell the difference between a 'real-life' event and an 'imagined' one. Waitley used the power of visualization to help athletes strengthen the neural pathways used in their sport.

Camille Duvall, five-time world champion and Hall of Fame water skier said, "*I train myself mentally with visualization. The morning of a tournament, before I put my feet on the floor, I visualize myself making perfect runs with emphasis on technique, all the way through to what my personal best is in practice. The more you work with this type of visualization, especially when you do it on a day-to-day basis, the more you'll begin to feel your muscles contracting at the appropriate times.*"

Modern research, such as that by Ursula Debarnot[xiv] at the University de Genéve, showed that changes that occur in the brain during mental practice were found to closely mimic those observed during physical practice.

Children are being taught to use visualization to improve their performance in diverse activities, from football to dancing. Coaches teach young footballers to visualize kicking, catching and goal scoring skills, modelling the activities of football greats. Instructors teach dancers to go through the entire routine in their heads, seeing it perfectly performed.

Air Force Colonel, George Hall, a four-handicap golfer, was also a POW for seven years during the Vietnam War. Locked in his cell he played a full game of golf in his imagination every day, visualizing every hole, stroke and putt. After his release, he played in the New Orleans Open and shot a 76, four over par.

Medicine

Studies have proven that visualization enhances surgical technical skills for doctors operating on patients. One study[xv] found mental practice before performing the surgery improved the result by 30% and performance was better with a thinkualization (both visual in "seeing" the activity and kinesthetic in feeling it).

Dr. Teodor Grantcharov, a surgeon in Toronto, uses the technique to optimize his operating room performance. Dr. Grantcharov is quoted as saying[xvi] "*... I think for five to ten minutes about the cases I have today and kind of imagine* *what kind of steps am I going to do. What am I going to do if this goes wrong? And it kind of prepares you mentally for the day. And suddenly I feel less stressed. I still do it every day when I'm in the operating room."*

Engineering

Nikola Tesla, Serbian-American engineer and physicist born in 1856, and the inventor of the AC electricity supply system we use today, would visualize countries, cities and people at an early age, teaching himself how to visualize. Later, Tesla would visualize an invention in his mind with extreme precision, including all dimensions, with no models, drawings or experiments, before moving to the construction stage. Tesla obtained around 300 patents in his lifetime.

Music

Musicians use mental practice in learning to master a musical instrument or a piece of music. Legendary classical music pianists Arthur Rubinstein and Vladimir Horowitz practiced in their heads, Horowitz to avoid using a piano other than his own and Rubinstein as part of his daily practice. Neurological researchers studied mental visualization for music practice.

Other

Visualization used in the mental practices of the Buddhist monks allows them to reach mental states and perform physical acts that are astounding to most of us. This has also been the subject of study by a number of university researchers.

Weight Loss

In most cases, except for some medical cases, your weight is due to your choices – what you eat, how much and how often, and what exercise you get. If you want to change your weight, you change your behavior. The mental image you have of yourself, and how you think, will influence how you approach this change. You have two choices – think about how overweight you are or think about how you will be once you reach your ideal weight.

Which one will motivate you to eat well and exercise regularly? Will thinking about how you will look, what clothes you can buy, how people will relate to you and what activities you will be able to do, motivate you more than thinking about the fact that you are not at your required weight? Think how you will be when you are at your ideal weight because thinkualizing where you *want* to be calls you to action to get you there. This will work whether you want to lose weight for your health or gain weight to increase your muscle bulk.

Focusing on the outcome, rather than the problem, is a good technique, as it creates the awareness for identifying the opportunities for solutions and identifying the path to achieving the outcome.

Health

What you think about your health does influence your health. It will influence the decisions you make about what you eat, whether you exercise and what medical attention you will seek. If you think positively about your health and desire to be healthy and fit to enjoy life, you might make choices not to eat fatty foods, you might decide to get out of bed earlier and go for a run, to reduce your alcohol intake or to follow up with a medical practitioner any ailments you have. The key here, again, is action. You think about the desired state (better health) and if you want it enough, you will take action to achieve it.

PLY: *Dr X suffered a debilitating illness and doctors couldn't do anything. "I started to look beyond medicine. Something just said, 'Look, you just can't be put here on earth to be this sick and there not be a way to get well.' I just wouldn't believe it or accept it." "I always thought I'd get well. Once I had decided that there was a way, there had to be a way, I knew, but I think it took, probably took about four years." This was a great achievement and Dr X had the confidence to be well, and then dived into the research to find the cure.*

Visualization also played a role. "It's one of those things where I found out a lot about my relationship with my body and what I do...a lot of it is what I do naturally."

There are documented cases of people improving their ailments through thought (the equivalent of "kissing it better"). Dr. Adrian Sandler[xvii] studied the effects of the hormone secretin on autism after recorded cases of improvements in children after they received the hormone. He found that the hormone did no better than a placebo (saline) but in both cases the children improved. Jo Marchant, PhD in genetics and microbiology and a science writer, documents a myriad of such stories from doctors in her book, *"Cure: A Journey into the Science of Mind Over Body."*

Mental techniques are used in pain reduction. In a journal article, Dr. John Astin[xviii] provides recommendations on the use of mind-body therapies (e.g., relaxation, meditation, imagery, cognitive-behavioral therapy) for the treatment of chronic pain, tension headaches and for improving recovery after surgery.

Research is increasingly conducted into the effects of the mind on the immune system, the treatment of cancer and the progression of malignant diseases. The effects of stress on health are widely known and well documented, as are mental techniques for reducing stress such as hypnosis, relaxation, meditation and neuro-feedback.

The effect of the mind and thinking can have a positive effect on one's health, both through the actions you take and the various mind-body interactions.

When I Learned to Thinkualize

Pain Control – When I was a kid, I suffered from what my mother called growing pains. I would get a pain in one leg that would keep me awake at night. I visualized and focused not on where the pain was, but where the pain was not. I focused on the feeling in the leg without pain and eventually the pain in the other leg dulled and I could sleep. Why did this work? A paper in the journal *Brain: A Journal of Neurology*[xix] reports that testing showed the intensity of pain reduced when the patient was distracted from the pain using a cognitive (thinking) task.

Pole Vault – In my final year studying engineering at university my friends and I decided to take Track and Field as an elective subject. We learned the basics of all of the track and field sports. We also attempted to learn how to pole vault (Google it if you haven't seen it before).

None of us had ever attempted to pole vault and we were not athletes. The instructor demonstrated the process; grip the pole, run towards the pit, change grip, drop the end of the pole into the pit, push forward as the pole bends, swing up as the pole takes your weight, push up over the bar, twist your body, push the pole away, roll onto your back and drop to the mat. Grip, run, grip, drop, push, swing, push, twist roll, and drop (GRGDPSPTD). Sounds complicated, doesn't it?

Then it came time to do what the coach taught. Some guys missed the pit, some couldn't get the height and some chickened out. I used thinkualization to go through the process in my mind, GRGDPSPTD repeatedly. I saw myself go through the actions, felt the muscles twitch and saw the view looking up at the bar. I started to run, went through the process and … up, over and a good landing with the bar intact.

This is the day I learned the true power of thinkualization. It was no record-breaking jump but I had trained my body to do what was required, correctly, the first time, by thinking through the process repeatedly. By the way, after that, many of the other guys performed successful vaults.

Action Statements

1. Thinkualize your goal using all of the senses, visual, sound, touch, smell and taste and even temperature and movement, with as much clarity as you can.

2. Write the thinkualization down. When you read it, you will refresh the vision in your mind and this will help you to refine it.

3. Internalize the thinkualization by associating with it. In your mind, you perform the actions and feel the environment. You are in the picture, not simply looking at yourself as if you are watching a movie.

4. At the end, step away from the goal and dissociate from it so that you are observing from the outside, watching yourself in the movie.

CHAPTER 7

Path Setting

CHAPTER 7
Path Setting

"It is not enough to take steps which may someday lead to a goal; each step must be itself a goal and a step likewise."
Johann Wolfgang von Goethe – German Writer and Statesman, 1749-1832

"To get to the mountain, focus on the mountain."
Chris Christoff

Imagine you are on a mountaintop and your destination is the mountaintop in the distance. Ahead of you are jungles and rivers, plains and rocky outcrops. As you proceed, your focus is simple – the other mountaintop. Each decision you make, whether it be to cross a river or take a path through the jungle or climb a rise rather than go around, is influenced by the direction of the goal ahead, the other mountain. All along the path, you have two things in mind – the path ahead and the mountain.

Small goals are stepping-stones to larger goals. Imagine the larger goal and apply the same technique to the steps, each of which becomes a goal to achieve on the way (e.g., cross the river, walk across the desert). You will weave your way across the landscape, taking the paths available, ever focused on the destination mountain. It is OK for you to zigzag to the mountain.

Now that you have set some goals and have mental representations of the goals to motivate and drive you, we will look at goal realization, getting on the path to achieving the goal.

The path is the engine room, where the guidance system comes into effect and where the work is done. The path is where you will excel, where you make all the necessary adjustments to get to the end, where you learn, have fun, focus and develop. Along the path, what do you do? You set goals. These are the sub-goals to complete the steps to the ultimate prize and the techniques for thinkualization are just as valid for use with the sub-goals.

PLY: *Joanne – "One thing I like to do and have done with some success, is renovate houses. You have to set lots and lots and lots of tiny goals and then day by day, day by day you have these little goals, you eventually realize the big goal and the whole house is done."*

In Chapter 2, I wrote about my personal experience in leaving the IT industry and becoming a property developer. My final goal was not well defined but it was enough to motivate me strongly. I thinkualized a new reality as the final goal and used this to generate the actions along the path.

Use the path to refine the goal as you learn and gain experience. Even if you have a firm goal, don't be afraid to refine it as you progress.

> **"A start, end and everything planned in the middle is a project. Life isn't."**
> Chris Christoff

The Path

For a long time, goal setting was a big challenge for me. I couldn't simply set the goal and the timeframe without understanding the path I would have to take to get there. Without this understanding, the goal was not believable to me. I envied those who decided what they wanted, when they wanted it by and went for it. I did notice that many of them didn't get to the goal and that helped me justify my thinking.

Then I had an experience that changed it all. I needed to get something done in a fixed time, no questions. I could not see the path, just the goal and the timeframe, and I achieved it. It did not mean I didn't plan, I did, and I had to take massive action, but I had to set the goal and believe I could do it (see *Obstacle Shopping List* later in the chapter).

Much like the mountain example, when you set the goal, the path can become apparent once you start to act, once you start moving. With movement, in any direction, you can steer. As you thinkualize the goal and the sub-goals, your vision becomes clearer, you will start to see opportunities related to your vision, and you will see different paths by which you might travel to your goal. This is path setting.

On the home building theme, you might notice advertisements for homes you normally would not have seen, see land development billboards you'd never noticed before, see furnishings you like, notice mortgage opportunities or talk to people about good builders. Your thinkualization will drive your actions. It is up to you to take the action.

A View of Obstacles and Opportunities

Even if the goal is not perfectly clear, working out the steps needed to take you in the right direction and identifying the obstacles along the way is a massive confidence building exercise. The goal-path definition exercise can be a loop, with a better-defined path leading to more clarity in the goal, which in turn assists with better path definition. You may "wobble" your way to the goal or to even make major changes to the goal and veer off on another path. This is all OK and part of goal achievement. You are more likely to fail to achieve a goal due to lack of effort, not lack in identifying the goal. For this reason, the path setting is critical for goal attainment.

Identifying the obstacles can also highlight new goal or path opportunities. Going through or around obstacles can reveal new ideas, expose you to new thinking or even bring new people into your circle to help you achieve. When visions and dreams are greater than any obstacles, the obstacles become opportunities. Behind every obstacle is an opportunity, so look behind every obstacle.

PLY: *Speaking about a mistake she made in business, Jacqui said, "I was blinded by the success I was having in my own private practice. So,*

essentially I focused on what I wanted to the point I could not see I was not focused on the WHOLE business."

Goals can also be too specific, focusing attention so narrowly, blinding you to important issues or opportunities. In a paper from the Harvard Business School[xx], the authors cite stories where goals that are too specific or narrow result in unintended outcomes and important features of a task being overlooked. Simons and Chabris demonstrate such blindness from focused attention in an amazing video, "The Monkey Business Illusion." Go check out the video for yourself![xxi]

Marc Miles is a trainer and a speaker. I bounced a few of my ideas off Marc and he has adapted them for his own use. Marc writes his goals on sticky notes, puts them on the kitchen wall and forgets about them. He knows they are there and he "sees" them every day. He is finding that he is seeing opportunities he didn't see before or wasn't ready for, meeting people who can help him, and realizing that some goals will only be reached through learning and development. Marc calls this "the power of the sticky note." Having some flexibility in the goal and its attainment allows you to realize a better outcome and can reduce the stress in getting there.

S. Truett Cathy opened the first Chick-fil-A in 1946 and by 2014, it became a $6 billion company. Cathy is quoted as saying, *"Many successful people I know set magnificent goals for themselves, then let nothing stand in the way of their achievement. I don't engage in that kind of long-range planning. Instead, I leave myself and my company available to take advantage of opportunities as they arise."* In an interview published in the New England Journal of Entrepreneurship, Cathy said, *"I feel like I never planned Chick-fil-A, it just came about. I say take advantage of unexpected opportunities."* This does not mean he sat around and let it all happen. His philosophy was "you got to want to, you got to develop the skills and the know-how and you got to do it."[xxii]

PLY: *Paul – "When gains or wins also occur because of specific circumstances – we all must be prepared to take full advantage of opportunities when they arise – this is the risk–reward process."*

The reason we build the mental representation of the goal first is, firstly, we need a reference point against which to plot the path and to evaluate the obstacles. Secondly, research has shown that psychologically the process needs to be in this order: build the vision and then evaluate the obstacles. You elaborate the desired future and then elaborate present obstacles, to get your commitment dependent on your expectation. You know you are more likely to achieve goals you see as achievable. Let's look at ways to identify the path and obstacles.

Big Goals into Small Goals – The Steps

> **"Arriving at one goal is the starting point to another."**
> John Dewey – American Philosopher, Psychologist,
> Educational Reformer, 1859-1952

Psychologist Karl Weick [xxiii] says complex social problems can be overwhelming, and argued for recasting larger problems into smaller, achievable goals that produce visible results. He maintained that through slow, steady progress, the strategy of "small wins" often generates more action and more complete solutions to major problems.

PLY: *Donna – "I started with 20 steps and had to stop at 24 or 25, and got to 30, and decided that amount, that's all I could handle at that stage. It took 11 months to train for this marathon. My first goal was doing a 5.3 Km run. That's all I was focusing on, that first step. Still, I always had the long-term in my mind. I never took my vision away from that because why I was doing the first step was to get me closer to the long-term goal, the big goal."*

Have you ever written down an item you've already completed on your to-do list so you can have the satisfaction of immediately crossing it off and experiencing the sense of progress? In their book, *The Progress Principle,* Teresa Amabil, Harvard University and Steven Kramer demonstrate how even the smallest, most mundane steps forward can motivate and inspire you to achieve.

Marc Miles, in striving for sales and performance targets, would often feel stressed (these are self-imposed targets, as Marc is a driven individual). Marc now breaks down his big goals into smaller ones (monthly targets into daily and weekly targets and activities) and focuses on these. He also says he is more relaxed and is achieving much more.

Let's look at an example of how you might decide on the steps for a goal. Continuing with the house theme, you have built the dream in your head, you've imagined walking through the house – you have a vision. What questions do you need to ask yourself to work out the steps along the path? Someone once said the quality of your life is determined by the quality of the questions you ask.

Let's assume you don't have $10m cash and that the first big step in getting the home is to save a deposit and get a loan. For this milestone, you build a thinkualization – you might see yourself sitting in front of the bank manager, with a check on the table for the full amount of the deposit. You are signing papers for a loan. You are proud of your achievement and excited to be getting the funds to build your home. You look down and see your hand signing your name using a fancy pen you bought for this occasion. The weight of the pen feels solid in your hand. (Remember to disassociate.)

Next, break the milestone into smaller goals. Generate questions by brainstorming anything to do with finance and write them down. Remember, when brainstorming, no idea is too silly to consider. You might ask yourself:

1. How much money will I need for a deposit and for a loan?

2. Where will the money come from?

3. How much can I earn and save?

4. How will I fund it?

Unless you have done this before, these questions will likely lead to actions to determine the answers. Let's look at 1 and 4:

1. How much money will I need for a deposit and for a loan?

    a. Action: Do some research on homes.

    b. Action: Talk to some builders.

    c. Action: Talk to some realtors/real estate agents about costs.

    d. Action: Talk to a loan broker

    e. Sub-goal – Get a plan and quote from the builder.

    f. Sub-goal – Put a budget together.

5. How will I fund it?

    a. Action: Look at the various finance options available to you.

    b. Milestone – In six months sign a contract with a financier for funds.

Write down all of the required sub-goals in the order they need to be done along with the actions you have to perform; these together will form **the path**. From this exercise, you might decide to save for a deposit for 6 months, earn extra money through working overtime or a second job and sell any unused possessions. At the end of the six months, you will apply for a loan.

PLY: *Joanne on writing sub-goals and lists – " [For] A big renovation project, the more you write down the more likely you are to do a good job of it and not miss anything, and stay on time and on budget because it's quite complex."*

Now the next step, as in any project management scenario, is to determine what obstacles are in the way. Here you might repeatedly ask yourself "what can go wrong" questions. Here are some ways to phrase those questions:

- What would cause me to fail? What else? What else?

- What situations would cause me not to do the tasks – I am hungry, scared, stressed, lonely, tired, overworked, distracted?

- How would my life be different if I don't do it compared with completing the goal?

- What is another reason why I might fail?

- Do I believe I will succeed? Why?

- When I think about what I have to do, what negative feelings do I experience?

For our home finance goal some of the answers relating to the possible obstacles could be:

- I don't do the research to find out what I need to do because I am too tired after work.

- I could fail because I don't get a loan. I won't get a loan as I am scared to approach the broker.

- I could fail to get a loan because I don't re-prioritize my spending and don't save the deposit.

- I fail to find out about building costs because I don't make time to call builders for an appointment.

As you answer these questions, you will generate a wealth of useful information, including actions to perform, other sub-goals and even some motivation as you work through the issues. This is not an exhaustive list and you will perform this exercise many times along the path. For example, there are things that can go wrong with the broker, the banks, the builder or your life but you can't predict them all and you tackle them when they arise, using these same tools.

Now, let's jump back to the start. We dived in with the milestone to save a deposit and get a loan. If you can, if it works for the primary goal, work out what the milestones are. These are the bigger sub-goals along the way. This may require some research, some consultation with people you will need for help and those who have done it before, and some brainstorming. These can also come from your assessment of the obstacles and working out the milestones will also raise other obstacles you can use as opportunities/actions, as you did above.

For each of these milestones you build a thinkualization. All of these thinkualizations build towards the primary goal. Milestones for the home goal could be:

1. Save a deposit and get a loan.

2. Choose and buy the land.

3. Finalize the house design, colors and fittings with the builder.

4. Construct the house.

5. Move into your new home!!

Implementation Affirmations

How do you remember to buy bread and milk when you get a phone call when you are on the way home from work? When asked, you probably think about where you are going to buy it and what exit or turn you need to take to get there. When you get to that exit, you then remember to swing by the shop. It is likely you are using the tool we are about to discuss.

Training to run a marathon required me to get out of bed at 4am and run before work. It isn't easy to get out of bed at 4 am for most of us?, We would much rather stay in bed and we can easily justify it – "just another 30 mins, then I'll get up," "just a few more minutes," "oh, it's too late now, I'll do it tomorrow."

As I lived two hours from where I worked, and worked long hours, it was 4am or nothing. So, at 4am I got up and put my running shoes on and went outside. No thinking, just do it. Whether or not I went running was not relevant, the only goal was to put my shoes on and go outside – simple, easy and not daunting at 4am. Of course, once I got that far, I decided, "well, I am up, I may as well run."

I got up at 4am through an affirmation, a "when something happens, do something" affirmation. "When it is 4am, I put my shoes on and go outside to run and increase my strength and fitness." I have used these affirmations throughout my life. Psychologist Dr. Peter Gollwitzer and others[xxv] researching goal setting call them Implementation Intentions and the idea has been adopted into NLP and hypnotherapy training. Gollwitzer introduced the concept in 1999 and research shows the responses to the obstacles, in my case staying in bed at 4am, can be automatic, requiring no thinking to get the required action.

I even use them for little things, like remembering to take my car keys – *"When I open the front door I will check to see if I have my keys to take me on my journey."* As I suck at noticing things I am not focusing on, like my wife getting a haircut, I cheat and create an affirmation. *"When I drive up the driveway on Thursday I will compliment my wife on her haircut, to keep our relationship strong."* That is assuming she did tell me she was getting a haircut on Thursday….and I was listening.

I use them as affirmations and, as I need a term for them in this book, let's call them Implementation Affirmations. They are like affirmations, where you state your intention to exercise a particular action, attitude, state of mind or skill to motivate your mind and program your subconscious. Many of you will be familiar with affirmations as a developmental tool, where you repeat aloud a desired state as if it has already occurred.

Some of the affirmations I have used for years include things like:

- My successful property business makes me proud and confident, and capable and willing to give to others.

- My daily meditations empower me. I feel the mental acuity and calmness permeating my mind.

- I love the strength and fitness I feel from my daily exercise and healthy eating.

Affirmations are to motivate, so create affirmations that are believable but slightly out of reach. You will demotivate yourself by creating an affirmation you won't believe, such as, "*I am getting stronger every day and I will be able to jump over my house in a month.*"

We are going to use these affirmations slightly differently to create responses to obstacles that might arise on the path to your goal. Implementation affirmations take the form:

"*IF/WHEN something occurs THEN I will do action/behavior <optional affirmation>.*"

Write down the IA and recite it verbally for reinforcement to create a subconscious link between the obstacle and how you will respond to it. Thinkualize yourself doing the required action; see and feel yourself doing it so that your subconscious is used to the idea of you performing the action. Taking control of the situation, you direct action or behavior toward your goal, helping the IA close the gap between setting the goal and achieving the goal. Once the situation is encountered (the IF part), it triggers the action or behavior (the THEN part). Gollwitzer's research shows that the link between IF and THEN makes the response immediate and automatic.

My IAs have the IF/THEN but they are also an affirmation, so they have an affirming statement at the end to remind me **why** I am doing the action. This affirming statement is positive and written as if it already exists, as you can see in the examples above.

Yeah, mine sound wishy-washy and I am sure you can compose better ones for yourself but they don't have to be works of poetry. You can reinforce any attribute you wish to develop in the affirmation, programming your subconscious until it believes you. The IF/THEN works and the affirmation works, the research confirms it.

Three Major Obstacles

The first milestone is to get finance for the home. For that, you need to do some research on the internet to find out what houses cost to build, where you can buy land and how much it will cost. You've identified that you may not be motivated to do this after work, as you may be too tired. Two of the three major obstacles for achievement are obvious, getting started and staying on track. The third, less obvious, is getting off paths that don't go anywhere.

Getting Started

The first obstacle is fundamental getting started. By adding the IA to the goal or sub-goal and specifying when, where and how to get started, you are more likely to achieve the goal.

Getting started may be a problem if you perceive that you don't have the right skills, you have habits limiting you (e.g., you have to watch TV for 3 hours every night) or have behavioral issues that slow you down (e.g., procrastination). You can use implementation affirmations to overcome them.

PLY: *Jacqui may procrastinate but acts after she thinkualizes her outcomes, "It works seamlessly. I never even have to stress. I just start actually doing it."*

The best way to get started is to do it, just start. You will be amazed what a boost that is. To get past your obstacle of being too tired we set an implementation affirmation to get started on the research:

WHEN I walk through the door after work THEN I will turn on my computer and type in at least one Google search before I do anything else, < because I always achieve my goals >.

Usually this is enough to break the mindset and get you going. The progress you feel from starting can keep you going. If you are tired, thinking about this IA will help keep you going.

Note that the trigger is an event that will occur (you will go home after work). I don't often use time triggers as they are easily missed (what if I get home later) and I would have to set an alarm to alert me of the time.[6] The action to be performed has to be related to your primary goal and the milestone/sub-goal.

This IA is based on an external trigger – walking through the door of your house after work. IAs can be based on internal triggers, such as feelings, and research has shown these to be effective:

IF I feel too tired after work and don't feel like doing anything, THEN I will turn on my computer and type in at least one Google search before I do anything else, < because I always achieve my goals >.

The IA is useful for getting started on an activity that may be scary or one that challenges your confidence. Earlier, we identified a possible failure caused by not having the confidence to call a broker. In this case, we can use an IA to boost confidence, using words to prime your mind, for example:

WHEN I need to make a call for my new home, THEN I tell myself I am capable and confident as I dial the number, because I always achieve my goals.

This IA uses the action required as the trigger, to make a phone call to the broker/realtor/builder, with an attitude affirmation to boost confidence, and in this case, an action (dial the number). You could shorten them by dropping the affirmation off the end but I believe it increases the effectiveness, reminding you why you are doing it. Create IAs for each of the obstacles and use them until they are no longer required.

---

6. With the 4am running example, I did use time, however, I have trained myself to wake up at the required time without using an alarm.

Staying On Track

The next major obstacle for goal attainment is staying on track. Internal and external influences can affect your progress and get you off track. IAs can help to suppress these influences. Without focus on the affirmation, other things get in the way and you can forget to perform the required action or drop the action for a more attractive alternative at the time.

With the finance goal example, there are a number of identified actions required, such as contacting the broker, getting quotes from a builder and talking to a realtor about land sales. To stay on track, create a clear list of required tasks, exactly who to call, a list of questions to ask, what internet research is required and what obstacles are to be addressed. With that list, you can write IAs such as these:

WHEN I have cleaned my teeth in the morning THEN I will spend 10 minutes reviewing my action list, <to set up my successful day>.

WHEN I have eaten my lunch THEN I will make at least two calls on my list, <as I am a strong and effective negotiator>.

Use IAs to reduce the effects of many different types of issues that can take you off track, whether they are inner mental states or external obstacles:

IF I am tired/worried/angry/fearful/confused/annoyed/bored/discouraged... THEN I will put that feeling aside and do 10 minutes work on my goal, <as I am flexible and resilient in conquering all obstacles>.

IF work/family commitments/issues out of my control delay me THEN I will focus on addressing them so I can get back to my goal, <as I am an effective leader>.

The finance goal requires the saving of a deposit that is critical to the goal and requires control of your spending to stay on target. A behavioral IA may be required such as:

IF I go to spend money THEN I will ask myself if this gets me closer to my home deposit, <as I am a brilliant money manager>.

You can also reinforce an action with other associated actions, e.g., reinforce the intention to go to the gym every week by planning to do other things on the way or by meeting someone there.

Of course, most important to staying on the path is to NOT STOP. Whatever comes up, the only way to reach the goal is to keep going. Use your goal, sub-goals and IAs to keep going. Dodge the obstacles and keep going. You may not know how close you are to the goal but if you give up you will never reach it. We have dealt with issues stopping you and in the next section we will talk about overcoming the unobtainable.

Overcoming the Unobtainable

Many failed projects and products have had to be terminated. The HD DVD failed to take off and was later replaced by Blu-Ray. Google Lively, to compete with Second Life, lasted six months. The HP Touchpad lasted 2 months in the market and the Ford Edsel, 1957-1959, wouldn't sell. There are many stories of entrepreneurs who invested millions in systems and products that never saw the light of day.

PLY: Sharon Jurd spent a year working with a software development company on a customer management system for her franchisees. They ceased development because the system had many problems and was not going to meet the critical date. It was better to stay with the existing methods than to introduce a faulty system.

Sometimes our action, activity or even a goal may be going nowhere and needs to be terminated. It is OK to change the path or the goal itself if it is not working out. The challenge here is to identify that the activity is not contributing to the goal, or that the goal is unattainable, and to disengage from it. An unattainable goal will use resources such as time and money better spent on achievable goals, and creates stress and frustration and reduces motivation, so it is important to identify and eliminate it. However, a balance is required so you are not giving up too early on ultimately attainable goals.

Often, we are attached to our decisions because we made them. Sometimes, as we value the outcome too highly, or overestimate our resources, or we don't see the task as unachievable. The consequence is that we will strive even harder to achieve the outcome and because it remains out of reach, demotivating negative feelings of failure arise.

In Chapter 4, we mentioned the Zeigarnik effect, our subconscious needing us to finish what we start. If we delay or drop a goal before attaining it, the automatic system in our subconscious has the tendency to experience intrusive thoughts about a goal. This system also keeps us trying to achieve when the goal is unattainable.

When a goal becomes unattainable, your subconscious will also provide you with signals that things are not going as they should. The negative feedback (from yourself or others) that you may experience includes sub-goals failing, continually missing your deadlines, encountering factors you cannot control or experiencing significant stress. You can use IAs to pick up on the warnings and change your path.

PLY: *Paul – "I always set what I term criteria for failure – this means I must identify two or three things that, if they occur, the project will be immediately cancelled. By identifying two or three things that may deem the project unsuccessful at the start you can minimize any wasted time when these occur."*

For the finance plan, you might be feeling that your savings for a deposit are not going well. Suppose your strategy is to control spending to save as much as possible. You might set this implementation affirmation:

"IF I reach the 4 month mark and have raised less than 50% THEN I will change my method, as I am a swift and precise decision maker."

If required, you might work overtime and sell unused items you own as an additional strategy. If you have been working extra jobs and hours but not controlling spending so there is no impact on your lifestyle, you might change to a more frugal lifestyle strategy until you achieve the goal.

Yulia's story

Yulia told me, "*If I can't achieve my goals in six months I drop them.*" Why? "*Life gets in the way.*" Yulia suspended her career in the finance industry to have a child and now she is a mother of a 15-month-old daughter. Yulia's biggest obstacle in the path of her achieving her goals is getting her daughter into day care (childcare). In Australia, day care is expensive and there are limited places and long waiting lists. Yulia's goal is now to get a childcare place and to focus on that. Once she has day care for three or four days per week, Yulia can focus on the next step. Sometimes the first goal is a step on the path.

Update – Yulia took action and has her child in day care and her focus is on recommencing her career.

Taking Action

The factor that makes the difference is one word – ACTION. You can think all you want but unless you take ACTION, there is no desired outcome. Equally important, the action is purposeless without the thinking.

Consider this story that I heard when I was a kid: It is night. A boy is wandering around under a streetlight looking on the ground near a bus stop. A man approaches to catch the bus and asks the boy what he is doing. The boy says, "*I dropped my bus money and I am looking for it.*" The man walks up and down the footpath under the streetlight helping the boy look. After a few minutes, the man says, "*The bus will be here soon, I will pay your fare.*" The bus arrives and the two get on. As an afterthought, the man asks the boy if he remembers where he was when he noticed his money was missing. "*Over there,*" the boy points up the road. "*So why weren't you looking there?*" asks the man. "*Because it is dark over there*," replied the boy. This story was obviously set in simpler, safer times but the lesson from this is still valid – do something, take action towards your goals and see what opportunities arise to propel you further.

PLY: *John – "Think about it – it's just a dream. Write it down – it's just a goal. Put a date on it, work out what action is needed, what people you need to meet and schedule these actions. Take physical, mental and emotional action."*

Thinkualize your goals, constantly keeping the images fresh, clear, and continually updated. By the time you reach your goal, because you've been there so many times in your mind, you will experience déjà vu, all over again. ☺

> *"I've been here before in my head so many times.*
> *To everybody else it's my first Olympics but to*
> *me it's my thousandth."*
> Mikaela Shiffrin, Reigning Olympic Slalom Champion (Sochi, 2014)

Obstacle Shopping List

Thinking about what you desire, with as much clarity as you are able, can provide you with a shopping list of what is required to achieve your goal. My shopping list example – My goal was to increase the equity in my house so that I could borrow more for other investments to earn a living.

The Goal: Renovate my house in 3 weeks to add value and then refinance it (through a Line of Credit (LoC)).

The circumstances out of my control: It was November, Christmas was coming and most tradies (Australian for tradesperson) and suppliers have a two-four week vacation; I was about to be retrenched at work and for that reason I had to have the LoC established before my income stream disappeared.

This was a time when obstacles became opportunities to excel. I didn't know how I was going to achieve the goal. I visualized what the house had to look like my outcome. That enabled me to see all the work that had to be done, all the tradies required, the negotiation required to meet the timeframe and budget and the project management required to co-ordinate the work. The work required builders, painters, plasterers, electricians, floorers and plumbers. I posted advertisements on a local trade website and negotiated with each tradie. The short timeframe meant no messing around and I needed people who could act quickly. This was my shopping list.

The result: Work completed on time and a significant increase in equity and an increase in my LoC. I doubled this money in 12 months and was able to eat. ☺

All of the obstacles in the way (redundancy, the time of year, getting tradies) were motivators for me to get it done as efficiently as possible to meet the burning need for the LoC. I have to admit there was an element of fear motivation in this goal, due to the timeframe and the imminent retrenchment, which helped, but my focus was getting all of the tasks done.

Action Statements

Set the path:

1. Determine the milestones – research, consultation, brainstorm, obstacle analysis.

2. Build a thinkualization for each of the milestones.

3. Do it again, break the milestones into sub-goals by brainstorming questions to ask yourself (and research and consultation).

4. Build a thinkualization for each one. The exercise will generate the required actions.

5. Do it again and break the sub-goals down into further actions. The sub-goals and the actions form the path.

6. Do an obstacle analysis, asking yourself the "what can go wrong" questions.

7. Sort out the actions and other sub-goals that you discover are required.

8. Schedule them for action.

9. Develop Implementation Affirmations where required, using the "*IF/ WHEN something occurs THEN I will do action/behavior*" formula.

Creating IAs:

1. Use the formula "*IF/WHEN something occurs THEN I will do action/ behavior because < insert affirmation here>.*"

2. Write them down.

3. Put them up where you can see them – the car is a good place if you drive to work.

4. Recite them when you see them, do this at least twice every day.

5. Edit your IA list as required, deleting them when goals/tasks are completed.

Take ACTION, DO!

CHAPTER
8

Setting
Timeframes

CHAPTER 8
Setting Timeframes

"A goal is a dream with a deadline."
Napoleon Hill – American Author, 1883-1970

"Life imposes some timeframes, but mostly you choose."
Chris Christoff

Timeframes are a necessary part of goal achievement. Setting timeframes for a goal and timeframes on the steps to achieve the goal, helps develop the sense of urgency to motivate you to action. Besides, if you want something, you want it sooner rather than later.

Life imposes some timeframes on you, such as the date of the marathon you are training for or when you will sit exams for a course, so your preparation fits into this timeframe. You may have goals aligned to a season, such as a weight loss goal by summer time, and these give you a little more leeway. With these goals, you know the timeframe and you can work back from the date to determine what to do and by when. With these goals, depending on the amount of time you have, a more disciplined approach may be required to the take the actions needed every day to meet the goal.

However, most goals have a timeframe set by you, so you have the luxury of making the timeframe realistic. You also have the luxury of setting the timeframe, which can be an approximate one rather than exact. In both of these scenarios, take care to ensure that there is enough "tension" to drive you so you do not procrastinate and leave it to the last minute. Leaving things to the last minute will cause either tension to drive you to achieve or too much tension to drive you to quit.

You don't need research to tell you that goals set in the near future are more likely to be accomplished than goals set further out in time, as are goals with a timeframe (that research has been done).

The key for any timeframe, imposed or self-determined, is to break the path to the goal into smaller tasks and these mini-timeframes become the focus. These smaller victories are easier to win and will make the outcome much less daunting. Knowing nearer goals are easier to meet, Sharon Jurd breaks five-year goals into three-month segments and focuses on the three months. Focus on the three-month period, set the actions each week, perform them and review them at the end of the week. Evaluate any incomplete actions and decide whether to put them back on the list or drop them.

PLY: *John – "It is not about time, it's about focus management. If you are committed and focused, you will have all the time in the world. If you are passionate, you turn up on time."*

Sharon will often set a goal based on planning and then shorten that timeframe. She knows most times she will find a way to achieve the new deadline. Sharon is an experienced goal setter. If the area you are setting goals in is not so familiar to you, Hofstadter's Law may apply – "It always takes longer than you think." This is often true in the IT industry I worked in.

The *secret* here is that you are setting a schedule not an arbitrary deadline. The focus is on the schedule, such as actions each week over a 3-month period. Set a timeframe for the primary goal (if appropriate to that goal – see *Discovery Goals* later) and then set timeframes for the sub-goals and actions. Even if you don't know the timeframe for the primary goal, because it is still to define itself, you can make progress with the sub-goals by setting times on them.

PLY: *Tony Gattari says timeframes are important, as they give clarity. Without them, goals become fantasies and wishes. "I personally like the pressure because I think the pressure gives me focus."*

Dr X says, "I actually like deadlines. I'm very good with deadlines... Sometimes, I need deadlines. Sometimes I have to be able to also just stop and not have any pressure around it, so whatever needs to happen, can happen....[Timeframes] can really help me get things done but there are some things that it just doesn't work for, like with [writing] a book."

Carol Wheatley – In property, time is money. While you are renovating you are not making an income. "So once we've made a decision, we don't dwell on it... We go to the next step, the next step and the next step."

This approach significantly reduces the opportunity for failure. If you don't meet the sub-goal deadlines or the task deadlines, you know something is wrong and you can re-evaluate the situation. If you don't meet the deadline, you know you have done what it takes to get there, reducing the impact on your motivation.

My planning to get into property was a schedule, a schedule of practice. The best achievers in the world practice – sports people, musicians, artists, performers and business people, to name a few. Practicing enables continuous adjustment of the actions to meet the intermediate goals and keeps you focused on the primary goal (and enable you to make changes to it).

Ask yourself this question every day: What is one small action I could take today that would move me closer to my goal? While focusing on the smaller tasks, ensure you don't get lost in the small detail. Keep your final goal in your mind every day to reinforce why it is you are doing what you are doing.

Let's revisit the house example and assume timeframes for the steps and assume you want to complete the project in 18 months:

1. Six months to save for a deposit

    a. Put aside $X per week

    b. Earn extra money through overtime, selling unused possessions

    c. Anything else you can think of

2. Two months to get finances in order and secure a loan

    a. Engage a broker

    b. Complete the application process

3. Two months to finalize the choice of the land and secure it

    a. Choose areas to live

    b. Look at advertisements and visit housing estates every weekend

    c. Choose a block and purchase

4. Three months to finalize the design, colors and fittings with builder

    a. Interview builders and choose one

    b. Work with builder to finalize the design and the build contract

5. Four months to construct

6. One month for unknown incidentals

7. Move into your new house!!

Some of these would run parallel to each other, such as talking to your broker and getting loan paperwork done while you are saving. You might also use that time to find a piece of land, a house design and a builder.

For this example, let's say this 18-month goal has these five major steps, each of which is divided into smaller tasks. Focused on the goal of owning and living in your house, you tackle sub-goal 1. With the sub-goal to achieve the deposit, each week you focus on each of the tasks to get there. Let the tension of each task drive you, while you celebrate in your mind the outcome of living in your new home. You can motivate yourself through charting the progress of your savings and putting it on your fridge to see every morning.

Notice task 1(c), "Anything else you can think of." This type of task reminds you to give yourself flexibility to vary your path and take opportunities to accelerate progress or improve an outcome.

If this home goal is self-imposed and the 18-month timeframe is not critical, you have some flexibility in these timeframes, so some may slip a little but you may achieve others early. The more you invest of yourself in each step, the more your excitement level increases, spurred on by what you are doing and what you are achieving. This will further motivate you and drive you on through any difficulties that may arise.

Discovery Goals

Where you are yet to discover the final goal and/or the timeframe, the journey is one of discovery. You can achieve this discovery through the techniques presented in this book.

My personal experience in leaving the IT industry and becoming a property developer was a discovery goal. I had no idea how this was to happen or when it could happen. I prepared for it without knowing the timeframe. When the opportunity arose to move into property development full time I was ready, able to see the opportunity and confident enough to take it.

The message here is that some goals don't have to have, or can't have, timeframes. You can't yet see the complete path or see all of the actions required to get there. Each step in preparation is an achievement worthy of celebration. As you prepare, both the path and the goal will become clearer and soon you can plan direct steps to your goal. You may not have envisaged how to achieve the goal until the end; such is the flexibility of the discovery goal approach.

Using this approach, the goals you set are preparatory goals. Using the property example, in the next three months you might attend four property seminars and each weekend attend two auctions and four open houses. As you learn more and do more, you focus your preparation as the path becomes clearer.

PLY: *Goals can change as you move down the path and as opportunities open up. Donna started out wanting to learn to run again. She sought assistance from a coach who said he would help only if she had a big goal – a marathon. Through the help of a mentor, Donna turned the marathon preparation into a fundraising event. Her success led her to speaking to schools and organisations. She is now writing a book.*

Dr X was on a discovery voyage to find a cure for an illness they suffered from. The fascination drove Dr X, "It was this extraordinary fascination as a doctor, a human being, that there are all these things out there I've never heard of or just there was so much to discover. My whole world just kept opening up, and opening up and opening up."

Paul says, "Circumstances can change – if projects are monitored, goals can be amended or changed as appropriate so that an appropriate goal is achieved even though it differs from the original goal."

A working paper from the Harvard Business School[xx] indicated studies have shown inappropriate timeframes can have adverse effects, such as short-term targets may lead to short term-behavior that damages long-term opportunities. Give yourself some leeway and keep the big goal in your mind.

Missing a Deadline

By keeping some tension in the timeframes, you will strive harder and this will help drive you. What happens if you miss a deadline? Firstly, don't beat yourself up about it. That won't put you in the best frame of mind to deal with it. Simply stop, look at the situation, analyze your options and decide on a new course. Review the reasons, review the path, reset the goal and press on. Note that the goal or path may change as a result and that is OK.

The review process may involve you seeking advice from a mentor or a professional. If the issues are insurmountable, the best outcome may be to stop and consider a new goal (as we covered in Chapter 7). Short-term goals and good planning will help you identify early on that you're going off track.

PLY: *In the tough business world Paul Moni comes from, missing deadlines can mean disaster. Paul says, "If deadlines are not critical then the rationale for starting any project must be questioned. Like a bad marriage, it is better to say no at the altar than to proceed, knowing divorce is the only outcome."*

Patricia – "If you don't meet a sub-goal, it's like you're traveling along on this road to tick off the steps, then you've got to look for a way to compensate so the final deadline can be achieved."

Donna – Donna's timeframe for running the 10km slipped. "Sometimes you're not going to get to your date and can be disappointed by that. Things are going to get in the way. I had injuries along the way and my brother passed away. Life's going to get in the way."

Graham's advice if you miss a deadline is, "Keep moving forward to the next step, then the next and the momentum will build."

Joanne on missing a deadline – "You live on. And if it's my fault, I own up to it and say I could have done that better, it wasn't my finest hour, what can I learn from it? Goal setting is decision making … just make another decision, which is to readjust your goal, or do you still need to achieve that? If not, let's move on to the next thing."

Tiffany – "If I didn't meet a deadline, I was forgiving and then set another deadline that would push me to accomplish it. I learned to be flexible with my goals and deadlines. I also learned to set deadlines that inspire me to get it done."

Action Statements

1. Deadlines, or timeframes, can be imposed on you or self-determined.

   a) Set a schedule not a deadline, set timeframes for the primary goal and the sub-goals.

   b) Monitor your performance with the sub-goals and tasks to stay on track for the primary goal.

2. Include the "Anything else you can think of" task now and then to give yourself flexibility to vary your path and take opportunities.

3. Keep some tension going to drive you. If you miss a deadline, review the reasons, the path, and the goal and reset the goal.

4. Use the Discovery Goal approach when the goal or the timeframe can't be defined yet.

CHAPTER
9

Constructing
Your Goals

CHAPTER 9

Constructing Your Goals

> *"If you have built castles in the air, your work need not be lost; that is where they should be. Now put the foundations under them."*
> Henry David Thoreau – American author, poet, philosopher, abolitionist, naturalist, surveyor, historian, 1817-1862

> *"Never underestimate the power of rewarding yourself for a job well done. Your brain is a hedonic little beastie."*
> Chris Christoff

In this chapter we will look at how a goal is constructed, how to word it to aid in its achievement and to stimulate the subconscious and conscious actions.

SMART?

SMART criteria are commonly attributed to Peter Drucker's[xxv] Management by Objectives concept from 1954. George T. Doran published a paper in the November 1981 issue of Management Review where he proposed the concept of SMART goals. Many publications on goal setting have since used SMART goal setting (a Google search of "SMART goals" gives 27 million articles). There are many different interpretations of the acronym SMART, with the letters standing for different verbs and adjectives exhorting you to action. The classic interpretation is Specific, Measurable, Achievable, Results-focused and Time-based. This method of writing goals has its merits but it misses the mark in some areas and can make goal setting more difficult.

SMART says to set specific goals but does not say how you deal with non-specific goals or discovery goals, as discussed in Chapter 8. SMART exhorts setting a date (timeframe) for a goal, which at a high level is a good idea however, the practice of setting the time must be appropriate to the type of goal. It recommends goals be achievable but how do you know that until you try? It suggests you should play it safe and not bite off too much. As we know from path setting, the steps in the path are as much goals as the goal itself and are enablers to setting huge goals.

Phrasing Goals

Let's look at how to write goals. We will use the SMART concept as a framework. Here is an example of a goal my wife and I have set. We have land and a house with development approval to build two more townhouses. We intend to build the townhouses, keep one for rental and sell the other and the house. The goal is:

It is now 24 December 2017, I feel wildly successful as I drink champagne with Karen outside our development, thrilled about the "sold" sign on the two properties and our bank account showing the $100,000 profit and the rental income we will use to fund our next (ad)venture.

S – Simple – Write the goal in simple English, easy to understand and remember. This goal is also **Specific** as mine is that type of goal. Specific goals lead to better thinkualizations, better focus and ultimately, better performance. If your primary goal is not specific, you can use specific, milestone goals to achieve the less clear long term goals.

M – Measurable – Here you identify the last thing that has to happen for you to know you have reached the goal. We will have achieved our goal when we celebrate with our bank account showing the profit from the sales and income from the rental. In NLP terms, this is the evidence procedure. A goal can also be measurable in terms of tracking the progress made in the sub-goals and tasks. Phrasing the goal this way also builds in celebration, which we will cover later.

At the 2014 Sochi Winter Olympics, 18 year old Mikaela Shiffrin, slalom ski competitor for the USA, visualized herself standing on top of the podium. Shiffrin won the United States' first Olympic gold medal in women's slalom since 1972 and became the youngest gold medalist in women's slalom history. Shiffrin's last step, her evidence for achieving the goal, was to be on the winner's podium. This is what she visualized. Shiffrin's goal might have been, *"It is February 2014 and I am standing on the podium at the Sochi Olympics receiving the gold medal for the women's slalom."* Watch the YouTube video[xxvi], she almost fell in run two but recovered beautifully to win gold.

M is also **Meaningful** – The goal can be meaningful to someone else but must be meaningful to you, it must resonate with you and drive you. The dream of standing on that podium drove Shiffrin. For our goal, the profit is needed to fund the next venture. We know this goal is really a stepping-stone to other things such as financial security, the ability to help others, overseas travel, and nice cars and houses. It is for our next venture and adventure. This is our reason why.

You may have a weight loss goal. These are usually measured by the pounds/ kilograms you lose however, this number may not be a great motivator; it may not be meaningful. How about measuring progress and success by something you can do? You might try to touch your toes or to buy and wear a favorite article of clothing you have seen. Do these relate better than kilograms?

A – As if Now – The **A** is usually for Attainable but Chris Howard, the NLP practitioner, describes this well. He says to write the goal as if it is now the time in the future the goal will be realized, that is, it has been **Attained**. Write the goal in present tense language so that when you say it you are there, in your mind, seeing the outcome – associating into a thinkualization.

This is where a specific date can be specified, and is suitable for our goal. If we achieve the goal early in October 2017 or the time frame slips to February 2018, that is OK, the evidence procedure remains the same.

R – Results focused – Word the goal with the desired result built in. In our case, the goal is to build two townhouses, sell the house on the property, sell one of the townhouses, have a rental contract in place with a tenant for the second townhouse and to make a profit. The wording of the goal simply articulates all of that.

R is also for **Realistic** – If you make the steps realistic, the goal can be a bit out of reach. James Cameron, the filmmaker of Avatar fame, said, *"If you set your goal ridiculously high and it's a failure, you will fail above everyone else's success."* In any case, it only needs to be realistic for you. Realistic can also mean genuine, lifelike, convincing – it feels like you can do it.

If you want to chase audacious goals, take Astro Teller's advice and fail fast. In a February 2016 TED[xxvii] talk, Teller, head of Alphabet X (formerly Google X), says his team runs the hardest parts of the problem first, trying to fail the project, and they are rewarded for it.

You can look at your track record of success. If you always got what you wanted in life, make goals a bit more grandiose. If not, make them bit more achievable. As you create a record of accomplishment, and as you hit smaller or path goals, you can expand your primary goals. Nothing succeeds like success, as they say.

R is also for **Responsible** – This is where you can make the goal and its consequences safe; safe for you, the people around you and the environment (in NLP terms, an ecology check). This is where you take responsibility.

T – Timed – Picking up on the "attained" theme again, set a future date but in present tense language. Also, word the goal toward what you want, not away from what you don't want, for example, not "I don't want to be overweight" but "I fit into my new clothes."

When you word your goal, use this formula – It is now (date) __/__/__ I am doing/have received/own (evidence) _____ to (reason why)_____.

Go back and look again at my example. It is simple, specific and measurable (last step is to celebrate), as-if-now (written in present tense), realistic for me, safe for Karen and me, timed (24/12/2017) and is toward what we want to achieve.

PLY: *Joanne on timeframes – "You have to be prepared to be flexible and to adjust them, realistically. So the key in that is to build in a little bit of ... we basically call it slippage."*

Note the goal wording incorporates some or all of the attributes discussed above. It does not have to use all of them. If I were to write the goal I had to get into property development, it could have looked something like this:

"It is Saturday night, Karen and I are out to dinner celebrating the completion of my last IT project because on Monday I start working full time on a property development we have invested in, the first step to our life in property."

This goal does not have a date, as I could not set one. It required significant preparatory work, which did have dates. It required the right collection of circumstances to come about. It is simple, as if now, measurable and results focused but probably couldn't be classed as realistic as I had no idea how it was going to happen. There were steps to get to this point, such as the buying, renovating and selling houses which had timeframes that were often missed, and education goals with firm dates (for courses) but the outcomes were not specific.

Additional Goal Wording Attributes

There are some additional attributes to wording your goal. You already know that phrasing goals in a positive way and appealing to the emotions of achieving them (how they make you feel) will increase the success rate of attaining the goal. Oettingen and Gollwitzer[xxviii] and others researching goal setting, have labelled these "attributes".

Positive wording is a promotion attribute, which differs from a prevention attribute. For example, "I succeed at my goal" rather than "I will not fail at my goal." Goals that excite emotion are called intrinsic (internal) goals, which are different from extrinsic (external) goals such as getting a thing. The best way to get the thing is to understand what the thing will do for you and how it will make you feel (making it intrinsic). Researchers also define the attribute of learning or being skills oriented, where you acquire competence rather than simply demonstrate it. Promotional, intrinsic, learning goals tend to maximize attainment.

Let's look at a weight loss example because weight loss is one of the top goals for people. Let's say Olivia wants to lose weight. Olivia wouldn't say, "I don't want to be overweight" because being overweight is not a promotional focus.

Rather than saying she wants to lose 10kg in weight, she could say she wants to wear a new size 12 dress to the party in three months, look fabulous and impress her friends. The focus is on a positive outcome, timeframe and with a reason why. When she makes diet and exercise choices she will think, "Will this help me wear my new size 12 dress to the party?" The by-product of the goal is that she loses 10kgs or so, maybe a little less or a little more, and still fits into the size-12 dress.

The goal to wear a new size 12 dress to the party in three months, look fabulous and impress her friends, also has an intrinsic reward. When thinkualizing this goal, she can feel the excitement of attending the party, feeling and looking great in a new body and a new gown. The emotion accompanying the reward makes the goal considerably powerful. She is likely to stay at her new weight to enjoy her new clothes.

My development goal also has intrinsic motivation in the feelings it promotes. It is promotional because it is written in positive terms, using words of success and achievement. Although not expressed in the words, this is also a learning goal for us, as we will have to learn much along the way to attain this goal.

Mark Murphy, New York Times bestselling author, leadership guru and the founder of Leadership IQ, has researched the predictors indicating whether a person's goal will motivate them to success. Murphy's top two factors, accounting for 50% of the best attributes, are:

1. I can **vividly picture** how great it will **feel** when I achieve my goals – **43%**

2. I will have to **learn new skills** to achieve my assigned goals for this year – **7%**

Promotion, emotion and learning! All of the other attributes scored less than 4% each.

The New House Goal

Before we leave the house example let's look at how we might set goals and implementation affirmations for one of the sub-goals required to achieve the new home. Let's use this:

2. Choose and buy the land

   a. Choose areas to live

   b. Look at advertisements and visit estates every weekend

   c. Choose a block and purchase

Buying the block of land to build the house is in itself a major step towards the final goal. It is a significant goal on its own, constructed using the techniques for establishing goals. Achieving that milestone is also worthy of reward and celebration.

It is eight months from the start of our project and we are ahead of schedule. Our friends have gathered on our block for a BBQ to celebrate the purchase and we proudly talk about what we have learned, and what we will do with the home when it is complete.

This goal has a time period rather than a date and the end date has been modified along the path as the project is ahead of schedule. It motivates you to stay ahead of schedule. The emotion component comes from sharing the outcome with friends and talking about what it will do for you. From this, you can build a thinkualization of the event – *cars parked in the street and on the block, a white marquee in the middle of the block, the smell of the BBQ, the sound of conversation and the hush as people quieten for you to address them to thank them for coming and proudly describe your plan.*

You can relate applicable affirmations and IAs to the tasks required to achieve the land purchase. You have to research the areas where land is available and where you would like to live. When you find possible blocks, you will need to visit them and inspect them and the surrounding area.

Affirmation: *I research land options diligently and visit five blocks every weekend.*

IA: *When I get home from work, I turn on my computer and find five possible blocks, (optional affirmation).*

IA: *After breakfast every Saturday morning, I drive to inspect blocks and areas, (optional affirmation).*

The affirmation creates an expectation of performance. The first IA ensures you do some work each day on finding a site for your new home. The second ensures you get out in the car and look and, if there are no new options, you look at previous options. This will drive you to be diligent with the first IA to find new sites. Note: Write your IAs in the first person, as "I," even if you have a partner involved, as you can only take responsibility for your own actions. Once you achieve these goals, drop these thinkualizations and affirmations from your daily rituals.

The New Car Goal

We have referenced a new car as a goal so let's look at how we might express this goal. In this goal we will use the reasons why from Chapter 2.

It is 30 June 2017 and I am feeling proud and safe, driving my new Mercedes, immersed in the new leather smell and the music from the surround sound, to pick up my friends and go out for dinner to celebrate the success of my business.

In this example, the car is a reward for success in business. One motivator for the car goal was to be able to impress clients. The car is the evidence step for the business and taking friends to dinner in the car is the evidence step for the car goal. The reference to the radio and the leather add extra dimension to the feeling. Behind this goal would be a business goal. The car goal meets the need to be proud and not embarrassed around friends and clients. This goal is more of a performance than learning goal, although the business success may have had learning goals.

Celebrate

Let's talk briefly about celebrating your wins. I had lunch with a friend who is a trainer. In his profession, motivation and attitude play an important role but he said he still had problems with celebrating achievements. In particular, he feels guilty celebrating a goal achievement if it came easily. He was talking about major goals, not small tasks.

It is important to celebrate your successes. This practice trains your subconscious to know that when you set and achieve a goal, you will activate your brain's reward system and get that burst of dopamine, the pleasure-seeking hormone. In other words, you are conditioning your subconscious to LIKE goal setting and achieving. You may know what it feels like to exercise every day and then stop, possibly due to injury. You get a kind of withdrawal because you are used to getting the positive feelings and mental rewards exercise gives. I want you to feel that way about your achievements and success.

The reward should be proportional to the goal. For a small goal, such as a sub-goal or significant task, you might reward yourself with a couple of hours of TV or read part of a novel. This will only be a reward if you are too busy or too focused on your goal to watch TV or to read for pleasure. For a bigger achievement, you could reward yourself by allowing yourself time to go to the movies or dinner out. For the completion of a project, you might spend the weekend away.

You need to find your rewards. Movies, books, chocolate, visiting friends, a really nice bottle of Shiraz and hands-on renovating and gardening tasks (yes, really) are all rewards which I give myself when I achieve goals. Sometimes my wife and I will go out for breakfast on a Sunday, which can be a celebration for a small goal I have achieved.

PLY:

Sharon believes in the power of celebrating the sub-goals and major actions. Each celebrated success provides motivation for the next goal or action.

Patricia – "I'm very, very happy it's actually turned out well. The result of that, of course, is that it gives you a lot more confidence and then you go on trying to do other achievements. Expectation of success is always high once you've achieved success because you've experienced it."

Donna – "I've learnt to talk to myself like I'm my best friend. Acknowledge and celebrate after each accomplishment. Even after a long run, I would so look forward to running to the Gelati man. That is a small celebration to me."

The secret is to set the reward and take it once the goal is achieved. You will often be tempted not to take the reward because you're too busy and the next task has to be completed. John Gearon says he sets his tasks for the day and when he achieves them he does not come home and load himself up with more tasks, he takes some time for himself out of his business activities. John completes many activities in his day and as a reward, he stops work and does other things. This way, he trains his subconscious to work with him on the things he needs to achieve.

If you are good at what you do and a big goal comes easily, don't give in to the temptation to say it came too easily and therefore is not worth celebrating. When I asked my friend why a big goal he had achieved was too easy he said it was because he had already done all of the work, he had learned all of the skills needed and had put them into practice. I asked how others would have found the goal and he said they would have found it difficult. He should now reward himself for the successful application of all of the time and effort he put into preparing himself to be able to achieve these types of big goals.

The goal achievement does not have to be hard or perfect. I made good money in a development deal by simply investing. It was not hard but I had done a great deal of work leading up to that opportunity preparing for when the door opened.

Does the reward comes from achieving the results or spending the time, are you rewarding achievement or effort? If there is significant effort and you fail, should you reward yourself? Yes, you should recognize your effort and what you learned from the failure, in order to succeed. If the effort was significant, celebrate what you gained from the experience. However, as you now know, if you set up the path to the primary goal as a series of goals, there are many opportunities to celebrate. This is the way to reward effort.

Now I have completed this chapter, it is time for a cup of tea and something nice. ☺

Action Statements

1. Structure the wording of your goals around these attributes:

    - S – Simple, Specific

    - M – Measureable, Meaningful

    - A – As if Now, Attained

    - R – Results Focused, Realistic, Responsible

    - T – Timed

2. Use this formula to structure the goal – It is now (date) __/__/__ I am doing/have received/own (evidence) _____ to (reason why)_____.

3. Use this same formula for the sub-goals, with the evidence step as some small reward.

4. Word your goals in a positive way that highlights the outcome, focuses attention on the reason why and gives the timeframe.

5. Word the goal so it is Promotional, Emotional and Learning.

6. Find ways to celebrate the completion of large tasks, sub-goals and primary goals. The celebration should be proportional to the size of the accomplishment.

CHAPTER
10

Being Accountable, When to Share

CHAPTER 10

Being Accountable, When to Share

> *"Tell everyone what you want to do and someone will want to help you do it."*
> W. Clement Stone – Businessman, Philanthropist and Author

> *"The road to hell is paved with good intentions."*
> Proverb

> *"An improperly incubated goal can perish before it's born, if exposed to the elements too early."*
> Chris Christoff

What is accountability? Accountability is different from responsibility. If you are responsible, you are the one that has to carry out the task. You are responsible for the actions required to get to your goals. You are responsible for doing the work allocated to you at work. Accountability is answerability, to be able to answer for one's actions, to explain what was done and why it was done. You may be responsible for doing certain tasks at work but your boss might be accountable to management for the success of the project.

PLY: *Darren – "If you want to win, there's more to winning than just saying you're going to do it. You've got to plan for it and understand it and get the right people around you, sacrifice everything. ... If it takes three days and no sleep, get over it. If you've got to drive the truck and drive the race car and put the clutch in it and everything else, get over it."*

You are no stranger to accountability. Your boss at work keeps you accountable; company boards are accountable to stock holders, and politicians to the voting public. As I wrote this book, my publisher kept me accountable to the publishing timetable. You are accountable for your actions to your family, friends and the law of the land. Accountability, especially in the workplace, is often associated with negative consequences – it's your fault. This is not accountability, it's blame. Being accountable for your actions and for the goals you set is a positive experience in helping you achieve them.

When you are setting your goals, you are both responsible and accountable. You are accountable to yourself for your intentions and the actions you have committed to achieving. You may also be accountable to others involved in the success of your goal. You are accountable to your personal mentors, for the efforts they put in to guide you and their investment in your success. You may be accountable to business partners for the profitability of the venture you have undertaken and to financiers for the repayment of loans. Your goals will have an effect on your family and friends, as you take time away from them to spend working on the actions, and they may look forward to participating in the rewards from your venture.

It is valuable to have a mentor or an accountability partner to work through the week's or month's progress with you. Choose someone who will give you honest feedback, keep you motivated and provide ideas and inspiration for problem solving through the obstacles that arise.

Announcing Your Goals

A word on sharing your goals with others and being accountable to others: traditional advice will say to share your goals with everybody because this makes you accountable, putting pressure on you to perform. The idea is that you want to be true to what you say, save face, be responsible and not let anyone down. You are announcing your goal to the world and the world is now watching you. When it comes down to it, a goal is an intention to do something. When this is admitted publicly, it leads to a self-view with which your subconscious will try to act consistently.

You may want to consider **not doing that** initially because goals in their early stages can be fragile and if not properly incubated, they can perish before they are even born. There will be well-meaning people who want to protect you. They will try to discourage you from taking any risks and from "getting too big for your britches." This is normal because it is a normal function of your brain to warn you continually about risk. This is something you have to continually monitor and assess (or ignore). Their brains are telling them the same thing but they are not learning how to deal with those thoughts, so they bring them to you as "advice."

PLY: *Jacqui – "I didn't go to university for my family. I didn't tell anybody. I didn't want any pressure....It was enough that I had the internal pressure on myself, that I was actually putting myself out there, to do that."*

Coral – "We started not listening to anyone because we wouldn't have done anything if we listened."

Secondly, there will be those people who want either to pull you down or to keep you at their level. As you set and work towards your goals, you will change. Others will see the change and you will get the "negative" from them anyway. Don't give them any more ammunition by sharing your goals with them too early, if at all.

Thirdly, the goal may change. As you develop it and see what is possible it may vary considerably from your original intention.

Instead, share your goals, dreams and aspirations with one or two trusted confidants or mentors. I only discuss them with myself to start with (yes, I have a conversation in my head, or out loud if I am in the car alone). I then seek guidance from trusted mentors when I have some structure I can articulate to them. Select people who understand achievement and where the prospect of your success does not threaten them (see *Chapter 11 – Do You Need a Mentor?*).

As the goal firms up, you've had good positive feedback and your confidence in the goal has grown, sharing with others at this point can provide you with more motivation. As people see you are determined, you are able to answer their concerns (or not let them influence you). When you deal with the naysayers, your goal will become clearer and your resolve to achieve it will be stronger. There is also research indicating that receiving positive feedback for announcing a goal tricks the subconscious into thinking that the goal has been achieved, reducing your drive to do anything. Be aware of this.

PLY: *Graham's commitment got him past the naysayers, "In everything everyone told me 'you can't do that,' 'you don't know how to do that,' 'you don't know anyone in Hong Kong,' 'you can't speak Thai'....just be committed."*

Releasing the goal to a wider audience makes you accountable to that audience for delivering what you said you would do (again – not letting them down, face saving). This is, however, dependent on the type of person you are. For some people, the consistency between what they say and what they do drives them more than it does others. You will know people who do what they say they will do and others who are "all talk."

Many people, when they see that you are determined and see your progress, will support you and want to talk to you about your goal, your progress and how you are doing it. I experienced this while writing this book. As I answered peoples' questions, the concepts and ideas became clearer in my own mind. In talking about it, I was effectively teaching the concepts. To quote the old Latin principle, "*Docendo Discimus*" – "By teaching, we learn." Talking about the book also promoted the product, with many people saying this book was exactly what they needed. Talking about it brought helpful people forward, which resulted in me finding my publisher and receiving great advice along the way. Success breeds success and people want to be along for the journey with people who are achieving.

I chose the W. Clement Stone quote and the proverb at the beginning of this chapter as they represent the two positions on announcing your goals.

PLY: *Sharon will only reveal a new goal to a trusted few. A substantial corporate goal narrowly avoided compromise when information was leaked prematurely. However, Sharon says it is important to get the goal out there as quickly as possible as other people will want to come with you on the journey and you can't do it all yourself.*

Tony has a different view. Tony sees embarrassment as a tactical motivator. He says, "You've got to spread it out there. I reckon you've got to make sure it's highly visible because if you keep it to yourself, you can fool yourself."

Donna Campisi says, "Look, if you want to set a goal and achieve your goal and get away, start a Facebook page. You become accountable through so many people. By saying out loud, people have heard it … I don't like to go back on my word. That's what actually keeps me going as well."

As an example, you might want to save for the deposit on a home. Once you have saved some you could post on Facebook that you have 15% of the funds you need and update this number as you progress (or break the amount into 26 steps and refer to them as A to Z so you are not revealing actual dollars). You will probably find people encouraging you, making suggestions to make or save money and offering you cash instead of gifts at Christmas and birthdays. If you don't want to make the saving goal public, put a chart on your fridge at home to share with family and friends who visit.

There are cases when you want the goal to get out there to the widest audience, so people can participate in the journey with you. Some might be customers at the end, such as when writing a book or developing an apartment building. You may want publicity for the journey or the outcome to engage others, so you produce a better product or better financial returns. Some may come on the journey with you to assist, advise or even to learn from you.

When I trained for a marathon, I would train using a running tracker on my smartphone and I posted the results on Facebook along with a commentary of the day's training session. From this, I received positive feedback and I knew there were people who were simply watching to see what would happen.

Posting my results motivated me to rise early five days a week and train. It motivated me to not let others down who were supporting me or admired my effort.

PLY: *Donna Campisi talking about the doubters – "I want to run a marathon, I want to do it for the Royal Children's Hospital. 'Oh yeah, okay let's see if she does this. Let's watch her.' People like to watch negative dramas. It's like watching a car accident, people just have to stop and watch it.... But I was encouraging people along the way. One woman, [said that] when she saw me, it gave her the incentive to get off the couch and start running again. She inspired me and I inspired her."*

I used the training time to think through my training and life goals and my affirmations, to provide further reinforcement for why I was doing this. My Facebook timeline allowed me to revisit my journey to the goal and measure how far I had progressed, a small celebration.

Team

Sharing can also help build a team around you as you can't do it all on your own. Seek out those with the skills you lack but are required for you to complete your goals. Seek out the experts – even if you can't afford to pay them, see if you can get some time with them. There is a secret to this. Do you want to know what it is? The secret is … ASK. I interviewed some busy and successful people for this book, people whose time is worth hundreds or thousands of dollars per hour. I asked them if I could interview them and I asked for 30 minutes of their time. Invariably, I got far more than 30 minutes, something for which I am exceptionally grateful. However, sometimes you will have to pay for good advice, but it is worth it.

Expressing gratitude[7] to, and appreciation for, people that help and support you builds bonds and enhances your success team.

Choose team members who know what you are trying to achieve as well as some who have done it. In the property industry, I want an accountant and a

---

7. There is some interesting research into the effects of feeling gratitude – see The Last Chapter resource on the website.

lawyer who own property and have clients who own property. I want a financial advisor who's richer, from property, than I am. Choose team members who have your interests and success at heart (beware the accountant with the fancy office). In the development company I contract to, we all have money in the projects, we all have "skin in the game" so we are working for each other's interests and our own.

PLY: *Coral – "So I think it's important you find professional people. We've got a huge team of amazing people and they all think like us. They all have our interest at heart, they have integrity."*

John says, "Rule 1: I never take advice or feedback from someone who is unaware, unskilled, unknowledgeable or not better at the subject matter than myself.

Rule 2: I never take nutritional advice from someone who has more body fat and less energy than me."

Gai says, "If there's one thing I'm good at, it's networking and talking … If you just sit back and think that it's going to grow of its own accord, it's never going to happen. We're always trying to come up with new ideas and we've formed alliances with other people."

Action Statements

1. Goal progress review

    a. At the end of the week (or month), review your actions and compare your outcomes against your intentions for that week. Are you accountable for what you said you would do?

    b. Look at which outcomes you achieved and why they were successful, what you learned and what you could do again.

    c. For the ones that slipped – were they required, what stopped you and what you can do to rectify the situation?

    d. Answer to yourself on your progress for the week. Are you happy with your progress? What is the plan for next week?

2. Initially share your goals with only trusted confidants or mentors.

3. Ensure a goal is well incubated before sharing it widely.

4. When you have confidence in the goal, sharing with others can provide motivation, make you accountable and encourage others to help you.

5. Attract others to your journey to help you build a team.

CHAPTER
11

Do You Need a Mentor?

CHAPTER 11

Do You Need a Mentor?

> *"Mentors, by far, are the most important aspects of businesses."*
> Daymond John – American entrepreneur, investor, television personality, author, motivational speaker, 1969-

> *"Think of mentors as teachers, they will come and they will go. Some are lifetime guides for the whole journey, most are not."*
> Chris Christoff

Mentors

Mentoring is about having a role model who demonstrates methods, mindset or other traits that help you achieve your outcomes. You may have several mentors, some in person working with you and some observed from afar whose ideals and ideas you take on. Each of those mentors has qualities you admire and teachings you believe will help make you the person you wish to be. You have no desire to become them, you must be yourself, but copy from them what you need, to become the person you aspire to be. We are used to copying. It is how we learned as children and it is what we do when we are coached in learning a skill (sport, language, dance, math, etc.). We copy people every day by mirroring their body language to develop rapport when communicating.

PLY: *Jacqui – "Find someone that has faith in you. You have to find someone that believes in you... because there's lots of people out there that will believe in you and they are willing to listen and they will support you".*

Gai had someone believe in her to give her a start in business, "It was a difficult time for lending to women and I had no money and no assets. We were paying off a house but I certainly didn't have properties or shares or anything behind me and I had three very young children."

The lessons from a mentor can be categorized into characteristics (role model) or information (sage). The role model is someone you want to learn to be like, to take on behavioral and character traits of that person. The sage is one with wisdom and information and can teach you how to do things. A good mentor can provide you with both lessons.

PLY: *Joanne – "With property, I have a fantastic coach who I found through a mentoring program. ... I still talk to my coach every week ... that's a fantastic resource."*

A mentor(s):

- Sets a bar for performance that you strive to reach and in so doing, you grow and develop.

- Is someone you get advice from, bounce ideas off and with whom you share your progress and plan future actions.

- Is someone whose characteristics and skills you can copy.

- Will be relevant to where you are in your personal development and what you are striving to achieve.

- Will change as you learn and develop and as your goals change. You can expect to change mentors, just as you moved between teachers at school. You may also have several mentors at the same time, as models for different areas of your life.

- Or coach, is important for accelerating your development and ensuring that you don't have to make every mistake yourself. You will make mistakes, it's part of the process. You will also learn from those mistakes; however it's cheaper if you can also learn from others' mistakes.

- May be older or younger than you are. What matters is what they can teach you and how they can guide you.

- Is someone who will believe in you until you are ready to believe in yourself.

- Can help you resolve problems that you get yourself into or advise you before you get into trouble.

- Can open doors and introduce you to useful people to accelerate your progress.

- Is someone who has done what you are trying to do or has reached similar goals and knows what it will take to get you there. They can provide advice on what they did that worked for them, and what didn't work, and be there to plan strategies with.

- Will guide you to develop your own solutions and solve your own problems.

- Can help keep you motivated, especially through the difficult times. They can push you a bit harder than you would push yourself.

- Can keep you accountable for the actions and outcomes you agreed to.

Who Has Mentors?

Many, I would say most, successful people, regardless of their field of endeavor, have mentors. Richard Branson is quoted as saying, *"I wouldn't have got anywhere in the airline industry without the mentorship of Sir Freddie Laker* (founder of Laker Airways)."

CHAPTER 11: Do You Need a Mentor?

Many Nobel Prize winners, from economics to physics, had mentors. In the business world, Warren Buffett (CEO, Berkshire Hathaway) had a university professor as a mentor. Marc Andreessen, an American entrepreneur and software engineer is the mentor to Mark Zuckerberg, CEO and cofounder of Facebook. Apple founder, Steve Jobs, later mentored Zuckerberg.

PLY: *Dr X had to re-sit a chemistry exam. Another student challenged Dr X to study and he'd test Dr X on what was learned each day. Dr X got an A for the exam. While on a medical elective overseas, Dr X met a very good teacher. Under his guidance, Dr X sailed through the medical finals. "It was very important having people who showed me another way of learning."*

Robert Thirsk, Canadian engineer and physician, and a former Canadian Space Agency astronaut, has arguably the greatest ice hockey player of all time, Bobby Orr, as his mentor. Astronaut and former U.S. Senator, John Glenn, was mentored by his high school civics teacher.

Sports people trying to improve their game have coaches. In sport, there are many mentors. To name two – Phil Jackson, one of the most successful NBA coaches, was mentored by other NBA coaches and famous Australian Rugby League coach, Wayne Bennet, is a mentor to many players and was heavily influenced as a player by his coach.

PLY: *Donna – "Talk to people who've already done it." Donna has had a list of mentors who were needed at that time in her life, starting with her parents, her brother, the rehabilitation physiotherapist, her running coaches and the businessman who guided Donna in her fundraising.*

Mentors have been around for a long time, with Christiaan Huygens (17th century astronomer) mentoring Gottfried Leibniz (the father of calculus).

In the creative arts, many successful authors, songwriters, performers and actors had mentors. Isaac Asimov (science fiction writer) was mentor to Gene Roddenberry, the creator of Star Trek. Actor Johnny Depp was mentored by Marlon Brando and Leonardo DiCaprio has Martin Scorsese as his mentor.

Maya Angelou (author, poet, and civil rights activist) mentored Oprah Winfrey. Oprah said of Mary, *"She was there for me always, guiding me through some of the most important years of my life. Mentors are important and I don't think anybody makes it in the world without some form of mentorship."*

Many former world leaders, including Australian Prime Ministers and US presidents have had mentors. Charles J. Ogletree Jr., Harvard Law School professor, was a mentor to Barack Obama (44th US President). Democratic Lt. Gov. Bob Bullock was mentor to George W. Bush (43rd US President). Sir Robert Menzies (12th Prime Minister of Australia) was a mentor to Malcolm Fraser (22nd Prime Minister of Australia) and Harold Holt (17th Prime Minister of Australia). Many US presidents have been mentored by previous presidents.

In these examples, you can see both the role model and the sage. Bobby Orr didn't teach Robert Thirsk ice hockey, so was likely a role model. Martin Scorsese sees actors from the other side of the camera but likely teaches DiCaprio the technicalities of acting from the director's view and performs as a role model. Sports coaches teach the technicalities of the game and can act as a role model for off and on field behavior.

No matter what the profession, good people look for good mentors. Most successful people, if asked, will usually provide one name of a person who influenced their success; however, they usually have a network of people who mentored them through their careers. With today's technology, virtual mentors are available where you can meet across the internet.

Many people also have mentors they have never met, whose activities they study to inspire them. They read their books and watch their videos or attend their seminars. I think in the true sense these are not mentors, as there is no two-way communication. They still can be role models with characteristics to aspire to or sages with a wealth of information on a subject. Let's call them non-participatory mentors.

PLY: *A number of those I interviewed have non-participatory mentors:*

Tony – "I wouldn't say that I would have a mentor but I have been influenced, dramatically, by the achievement of others and I've been influenced dramatically by, essentially, the experience of life."

John says he doesn't have personal mentors. "I do like biographies and I always pull different methods out of those stories. I pick whatever they are the most congruent in and I take the perfect person and model those congruencies."

Tiffany – "I began listening to personal development gurus such as Jim Rohn, Tony Robbins and Brian Tracy. These tapes focused on motivation, inspiration and empowering your inner self. Once I started listening to these tapes, I become hungry for more. I started learning about goal setting, visualization, positive thinking and so much more."

Jacqui – "I have mentors I've never met because I read their books and I listen to their tapes. Then there are mentors that I have met ... I've grown, and grown out of some mentors."

For techniques for getting a mentor, see "How to Get a Mentor" resource on the website.

PLY: *Paul – "Good mentors are fantastic – those who spend time with you and work with you to overcome your lack of experience and provide encouragement for you to make decisions are the best."*

"I was fortunate to have a number of good mentors. [Some of] the key lessons I learnt include:

- *Have confidence to question or challenge things – respectfully.*

- *Have no fear in making a mistake – If you make a mistake, recognise this and seek to fix the error.*

- *Surround yourself with smarter people than yourself*

- *Communicate openly with people – people will reciprocate.*

- *Respect people – they will reciprocate."*

Thought Experiment in Self Mentoring

> *"Practice does not make perfect.*
> *Only perfect practice makes perfect."*
> Vince Lombardi

> *"We have all a better guide in ourselves, if we would attend to it, than any other person can be."*
> Jane Austen -19th Century English Novelist, 1775-1817

What if you could create a mentor in yourself, a perfect role model to show you what the outcome you want looks like? I call it Nisi, from omniscient (all knowing). Let's see how this might work.

Various psychology theories have used the term self-actualization, the top of Abraham Maslow's hierarchy of needs. Many believe Maslow's theories are outdated however, the traits of the self-actualized are useful to reflect on – they are not dependent on external influences, they value solitude (alone but not lonely) and they have profound interpersonal relationships with a few intimate friends. They appreciate the world around them, are true to themselves, have a driving mission in life to solve problems external to themselves, are able to judge situations correctly and see the world as it is.

PLY: *Tony – "I'm an avid reader and essentially, I am a person that would consistently challenge myself. I think it's called self-actualization, where you actually look from within yourself and ask yourself those questions."*

Imagine Nisi as a force that can influence you, inside you, not external to you. Imagine this force is the "perfection" you seek. This is not a replacement for a true mentor but is a technique you can use every day.

Nisi has no limitations, no physical, emotional, psychological or social limitations. Nisi has no fears, hang-ups or baggage. Nisi never experiences embarrassment or feels guilt. Nisi is always confident and appropriately assertive. Nisi always knows what to say, can communicate with people from every sphere of life and can command attention in any group. Nisi is positive and generous, creative, knowledgeable, intelligent and empathetic. Nisi is the ideal leader, manager, parent and diplomat.

Imagine the ideal you, if you could be everything you want to be. When you want to achieve something, whether it be a pay rise or the poise and grace to feel comfortable with the rich and famous, imagine how Nisi would do it. Imagine the scenarios, the interactions, and the outcomes with no limitations.

The subtlety here is if you imagine that *you* are doing it, you will be thinkualizing and you will experience the emotions that would arise in the situation and you will impose your limitations on the scenario. By imagining Nisi doing it, there is no emotion, just a "mental video" of how it should be done, which becomes your model. You then attempt to live up to that model (now the emotion starts), both in your imagination and in action, knowing how it should be done, referring back to the model as you go. Imagine the scenario with yourself doing it just as Nisi does, without thought of any limitation, judging or second-guessing. Just do as Nisi does.

You can do this for various scenarios, both those that are yet to come and those you have previously experienced but wanted the outcome to be different. Both of these exercises will develop a repertoire, a library in your head, to call on to provide the actions, words and positive feelings you need to handle the situation and achieve the desired outcome. As you become more comfortable, use Nisi to get to the next level. You can also "rewrite" the day's activities into a "this is how it should have gone" context – see *End of day Reframing* in *The Last Chapter* resource on the website.

Whenever you are going into a situation that is unfamiliar or stressful, you can thinkualize how you will behave and how you want it to go. I found this useful for job interviews or when I had to have a disciplinary talk with an employee.

Nisi's actions will be limited by your imagination but that is a small limitation, which reduces as you learn from your own experiences and from other mentors and incorporate them into yourself.

I encourage you to try this experiment on yourself and let me know the results.

Action Statements

1. Using an interview to approach a mentor:

   a) Research them on the internet. Read anything they have published and watch any interviews you can find. Find key points about them that you can use to trigger their interest when you approach them.

   b) Make a list of questions you want to ask in the interview. If they ask for the questions before agreeing to the interview, then email them (they will be better prepared).

   c) Ask them for 30 minutes of their time.

   d) Tell them you will be recording the interview so you can have it transcribed.

   e) After the interview have some extra questions to cover in email, as it is an opportunity to keep the relationship developing.

   f) Once you have completed the interviews, you can decide whom you want to approach.

   g) Work out what you want from them, being respectful of their time. If initially you get a no, then reduce your demand on their time.

2. If you know whom you want to approach:

   a) To make an impact the first time, send your first communication to them as a hand written letter.

   b) Each time you contact them, tell them what you have done for yourself, keep abreast of their work if possible and reference it.

   c) Always be respectful.

3. Develop your own Nisi

ABOUT THE AUTHOR

Chris Christoff

Author, Real Estate Investor and Developer, Project Manager and IT Professional

A fundamentally shy person, Chris has worked hard throughout his life to transform himself into the active and accomplished person he is today. To prepare himself to excel at university, he studied transcendental meditation. His mental focus helped him accomplish many goals, including developing a cardio visualization device, learning to pole vault using mental visualization, graduating in 1980 with a degree in electrical engineering, and completing an MBA in 1998 while working 80-hour weeks as an IT manager.

After university, Chris began a long and rewarding career as an IT professional. Chris built one of the Queensland government's first state-wide computer networks. Chris worked for various public and private organizations in IT General Manager roles, responsible for the development and operation of business-critical IT infrastructure, managing teams and departments and managing IT projects.

In his last IT role, as Project Manager for the 2014 G20 Global Leaders' Summit held in Brisbane, Australia, his work managing the design and installation of an IT infrastructure of 3,000 devices across 20 venues was formally recognized by the Australian Prime Minister. Chris also received appreciation from the U.S. White House Communications Agency for his work with the U.S. Secret Service.

Having purchased his first house back in 1984, Chris started a lifelong love of real estate. Chris and his wife, Karen, fully restored the old Queenslander and sold it for a 200% profit. Chris bought his first investment house in 1999 and dedicated himself to learning everything he needed to know about renovating. Over the years, he has studied property investment and development with many property gurus.

Always interested in self-improvement to counter his shy nature, Chris has also studied personal development and growth starting with the books, *"I'm OK, You're OK"* and *"What Do You Say After You Say Hello?"* in the 1980s. Chris follows the writings and seminars from many authors, speakers and motivators.

Adventurous and inquisitive, Chris has traveled and worked throughout Australia, the United States, Hong Kong, Vietnam and Fiji. Professionally, Chris is a member of the Australian Institute of Project Management and the Australian Institute of Management.

Chris Christoff is the author of, *"Goal Setting for People Who Can't Set Goals Proven Tools and Techniques to Achieve Anything You Want"* and lives on the Gold Coast, Australia with his wife Karen. Chris is now a full time property developer. Chris and Karen have three children – an IT project manager, a veterinary surgeon and an engineer. Chris is also attempting to learn Spanish.

Resources

GOAL SETTING FOR PEOPLE WHO CAN'T SET GOALS website

www.YouCanSetGoals.com/Resources

MY CONTRIBUTORS

Meriton Apartments

www.Meriton.com.au

Graham Bibby

International Investment – In the Business of Money

Richmond Group

www.richmondth.com

www.grahambibby.com

Theinsidersclub.net

Donna Campisi

Speaker, Writer, Workshop Facilitator, Humanitarian, Crazy Runner and Adventurer

Creator of Run Donna Run

www.rundonnarun.com.au

Jacqui Christie

"The Intuitive Psychologist," registered Clinical and Counselling Psychologist

www.rewireyourelationship.com

https://m.facebook.com/intuitivepsychologist

Carolyn Cranwell

Author *"Navigating Alzheimer's Survival Secrets of a Long Term Carer"*

www.Navigating-Alzheimers.com

Julius Czerny

Author, Presenter, Survivor

www.juliusczerny.com

www.superlifesaver.com

Patricia (Tricia) Dennis

International Author of "*Hell to Happiness – A Concentration Camp Childhood to a Life of Abundance*"

www.HellToHappiness.com

Tony Gattari

Achievers Group – Business Training, Business Coaching

www.achieversgroup.com.au

John Gearon

Outcomes Specialist

John@johngearon.com.au

Kawena Gordon

International Author, Clairvoyant, Speaker, Mentor

Author of the book "*Happiness Is Just a Breath Away – How to Achieve High Energy, Confidence & Vitality*"

www.expandingenergies.com.au

Sharon Jurd

Sharon Jurd Events, Business Growth Specialist

http://www.sharonjurdevents.com.au/

Tiffany Mason

Mason Coaching and Consulting LLC

www.tiffanymason.com

Paul Moni

Moni Solutions – Business Strategic and Operational Services

www.monisolutions.com

Darren Morgan

Darren Morgan Racing

http://www.darrenmorgan.com.au

Joanne Verikios

International Author of "*Winning Horsemanship*"

www.WinningHorsemanship.com

Coral Brian-Wheatley

International author of "*Building Wealth in a Self-Managed Super Fund – How I Turned 80K into 4 Million and How You Can Too*"

www.buildingwealthinaselfmanagedsuperfund.com

Gai Williams

Pharmacist and International Author of "*No More Tears – Colic Relief*"

www.nomoretearscolicrelief.com

USEFUL WEBSITES

Character Traits

I have listed a few in case some of them disappear.

http://writerswrite.co.za/a-fabulous-resource-for-writers-350-character-traits

http://www.fiction-writers-mentor.com/list-of-character-traits/

http://ideonomy.mit.edu/essays/traits.html

http://www.character-training.com/blog/list-of-character-traits/

This site has an extensive list of skills by career category

http://jobsearch.about.com/od/list/fl/list-of-skills-resume.htm

Find your own by Googling "character traits" or "Skills".

Transcription Services

www.rev.com/transcription

Want to Have a Dynamic Speaker and Trainer for Your Next Conference or Training Program?

Goal setting is a core skill for all levels of an organization, whether it is to boost sales, increase on-the-floor productivity, expand problem solving, meet project deadlines, enhance personal development or reduce fear and procrastination around performance. Chris will take your participants through the preparation phases to set them up for the best results, then through his innovative path, goal and timeframe setting techniques.

Chris Christoff has 30 years' experience in project management and IT management and is now in property investment and development. His methods apply to all aspects of goal achievement from corporate business, career, health and fitness, sports and finance to relationships and personal development.

Workshop formats are available to fit your program:

- Goal Setting Workshops
- Full or Half Day Workshops
- 2 or 3 Day Corporate Training
- Plus a variety of training options

Book Chris to speak at your event today!

Email: Contact@ChrisLChristoff.com

www.YouCanSetGoals.com

www.ChrisLChristoff.com

Imagine Achieving Anything You Want With Complete Control Over Your Goal Setting!

Enhance your Financial, Professional, Sporting, Business and Personal life with these extraordinary products using new, innovative goal setting techniques.

Enhance the skills you have learned from this book in the comfort of your own home, office and car. Explore the range of self-study programs, DVDs, audio CDs, books, special reports, interviews and reference material all designed to help you master goal achievement. Learn how to target and achieve all that you want in business, sports, health and fitness, finance, personal development and relationships, in fact, any aspect of your life.

Visit our website to view the full range of products

www.YouCanSetGoals.com

WORKS CITED

i. New Psycho-Cybernetics Updated Edition by Maltz, Maxwell, 2002, Prentice Hall

ii. https://en.wikipedia.org/wiki/Impostor_syndrome

iii. Imes, P. R. (1978). The Imposter Phenomenon in High Achieving Women: Psychotherapy Theory, Research and Practice, 15, #3(Fall 1978)

iv. http://www.news.com.au/finance/highachievers-suffering-from-imposter-syndrome/story-e6frfm1i-1226779707766

v. Dr Helena Popovic, author of NeuroSlimming, told Australia's ABC radio she teaches a similar technique for people to overcome diet cravings

vi. http://www.fastcompany.com/52717/change-or-die

vii. http://www.ornishspectrum.com/wp-content/uploads/dean-ornish-conversation.pdf

viii. W. Van Eerde, University of Amsterdam; P. Steel, University of Calgary; P. Gollwitzer, New York University, and others

ix. Steel, P. Arousal, avoidant and decisional procrastinators: Do they exist? Personality and Individual Differences (2010),

x. Dijksterhuis A (November 2004). "Think different: the merits of unconscious thought in preference development and decision making". Journal of Personality and Social Psychology 87 (5): 586–98

xi. Cleeremans A (2011). "The Radical Plasticity Thesis: How the Brain Learns to be Conscious". Frontiers in Psychology 2: 86.

xii.   http://harvardmagazine.com/2013/01/the-placebo-phenomenon

xiii.   Prof T. Greenhalgh, Role of routines in collaborative work in healthcare organisations. BMJ 2008; 337

xiv.   Experts bodies, experts minds: How physical and mental training shape the brain. Frontiers in Human Neuroscience. Debarnot U et al, May 2014 May 7

xv.   Mental practice enhances surgical technical skills: a randomized controlled study. Arora et al, Annals of Surgery, Volume 253, Number 2, February 2011

xvi.   http://www.theglobeandmail.com/life/health-and-fitness/health/surgeons-study-benefits-of-visualizing-procedures/article22681531/

xvii.   Placebo Effects in Autism: Lessons from Secretin. Sandler AD, et al. Journal of Developmental & Behavioral Pediatrics: October 2000 – Volume 21 – Issue 5 – ppg 347-350

xviii.   Mind–Body Therapies for the Management of Pain. Clinical Journal of Pain, Astin, 20.1 (2004), pp27-32

xix.   Imaging how attention modulates pain in humans using functional MRI. Brain, a Journal of Neurology Susanna J. Bantick et al, 2002 vol 125, pp310-319

xx.   Goals Gone Wild: The Systematic Side Effects of Over-Prescribing Goal Setting by Lisa D. Ordóñez, Maurice E. Schweitzer, Adam D. Galinsky, and Max H. Bazerman. Working paper 09-083

xxi.   (http://www.theinvisiblegorilla.com/videos.html)

xxii.   New England Journal of Entrepreneurship, Vol. 10 [2007], No. 1, Art. 5

xxiii.   Weick, K. (1984). Small wins: Redefining the scale of social problems. American Psychologist, Volume: 39, Issue: 1, Pages: 40-49

xxiv.   Strategies of Setting and Implementing Goals, Oettingen, G., Gollwitzer, P. M., Social Psychological Foundations of Clinical Psychology (Eds Maddux and Tangney). Also work by Sheeran P., Brandstätter V., Martiny-Huenger T., Prestwich A., et al

xxv.   Drucker, Peter F. The Practice of Management. New York: Harper & Row, 1954. Print.

xxvi.   https://www.youtube.com/watch?v=Kqj_u6cL0xs run starts at 5:52

xxvii.   http://www.ted.com/talks/astro_teller_the_unexpected_benefit_of_celebrating_failure

xxviii. Strategies of Setting and Implementing Goals, Oettingen, G., Gollwitzer, P. M., Social Psychological Foundations of Clinical Psychology (Eds Maddux and Tangney). Also work by Sheeran P., Brandstätter V., Martiny-Huenger T., Prestwich A., et al